RAMA IN THE INDIAN LANGUAGES

(Assamese Language)

RAMA IN THE INDIAN LANGUAGES
(Assamese Language)

Chief Editor

Dr. Yogendra Pratap Singh

Ex-Professor and Head, Hindi Department
Allahabad University, Allahabad

Editor

Dr. Anushabda

Assistant Professor, Hindi Department
Tezpur University, Tezpur, Assam

Co-Editor

Dr. Charu Goel

Assistant Professor, Hindi Department
Shyama Prasad Mukherji Mahila Mahavidyalaya, Delhi University

Patron

Sh. Jitendra Kumar IAS
Chief Secretary, Culture and President,
Ayodhya Research Institute

Sh. Shishir PCS
Director, Culture and Vice-President,
Ayodhya Research Institute

Visualisation

Dr. Yogendra Pratap Singh

Director, Ayodhya Research Institute : Tulsi Smarak Bhawan
Ayodhya, Faizabad (U.P.)

Vani Book Company

An imprint of Vani Prakashan Group

Vani Book Company

An imprint of Vani Prakashan Group

4695, 21-A, Daryaganj, New Delhi 110 002

Phone: +91 11 23273167 Fax : +91 11 23275710

India

Branches

Ashok Rajpath, Patna 800 004, Bihar

Coffee House Campus, Mahatma Gandhi Marg, Allahabad 211 001, Uttar Pradesh

Mahatma Gandhi International Hindi University, Wardha 442 001, Maharashtra

Motia Park Opp. Water Tank, Sultania Road, Bhopal 462 001, Madhya Pradesh

Goripur Taliya Para, 313, R.B.C. Road 24- Parganas (North) Kolkata 743 166, West Bengal

In Association with

ESTD.-1986

Ayodhya Research Institute

presents

RAMA IN THE INDIAN LANGUAGES : ASSAMESE LANGUAGE

Chief Editor Dr. Yogendra Pratap Singh

Editor Dr. Anushabda

Co-Editor Dr. Charu Goel

Visualisation Dr. Yogendra Pratap Singh

ISBN : 978-93-89915-49-5

Religion/Culture

First Edition 2020

Price : ₹ 495

Printed at City Press, Delhi-110 095 (India)

Vani Prakashan's signature motif is created by Artist Maqbool Fida Husain

EDITORIAL

Whenever there is a cultural lag in time and space, it often creates a crisis of cultural deletion. Today, the crisis is at its zenith. Although technology and technological advancement have accelerated over physical development, culture has been lagging behind in this competition; and civilization has gone a long way. Whereas on one hand, physical civilization seeks to enter into another solar system leaving the present one behind; on the other hand, we have gone so far from each other, that we are barely able to explore the happenings of our neighborhood. This insensitivity is giving us the status of being human robots. Although, civilization is the climate, culture is its vital air that makes our sensations palpitate, strengthens the spirit of humanity, thus proving us to be homosapiens. Though civilization has taken birth long back, when man learnt to produce fire for the first time by rubbing two flint stones against each other; it would be the day when we start respecting every one and is ready to sacrifice ourselves for the benefit of others. That's when the actual birth of human civilization would be marked.

Actually the end of civilization is possible, but an entire destruction of a culture is not possible. The reason being, civilization resides in thoughts, whereas the domicile of culture is in the sacraments. Culture runs in our veins and civilization through our body. This is why, no matter how hard the capitalist concepts like modernism, globalization etc. have tried to cast its evil spell over our cultural heritage, they couldn't even shake a piece of straw of its foundation. They have held their twigs so rigorously that it is actually possible to rebuild the nest. The only thing to be done is, to prevent the imported cyclones. I think there is no greater protective shield than 'Ramkatha' (story of lord Rama). 'Ramkatha' is that shield, which has instilled the idea of Rama in our existence. The reason being that, Rama and Krishna are the names of the biggest dreams of humanity. They shine in the pupils of our eyes and run through our arteries.

The roots of the 'Ramkatha' are very deep rooted, and its branches and sub branches are spread across the nook and corner of country, with slight amount of homologous disparity. Ram katha has its deep penetration across the continent of Asia. It covers a vast empire of the entire Asian population. In his research thesis, decades ago, Father Camille Bulcke has proved that Ram katha is not only an Indian fiction but also is an International one as well. This extension of Ram katha was referred to as 'Digvijay of Valmiki' by Father Camille Bulcke. The roots of this legend dates back to the 4th century B. C. But it is inaccessible due to being confined in the oral tradition. Ramkatha finds its place in the Jataka tales, by considering Rama as the 'Bodhisattva'. Inspired and influenced by Valmiki, Ram katha adaptations are found in different languages of India. Its clear impression is also found in the non literary arts of the country and abroad. Ramkatha's illustrations are found on the paintings and sculptures of Sri Lanka, Java, Sumatra, Cambodia etc. In Mauritius when our ancestors were punished with black water; it was the narration of Ramkatha (Ramayana) in the evening, that gave them relief and relieved them from despair and depression of the whole day's hard work. Ramayana was a tranquilizer for them. This life saving tale needs to be revived, in order to deal with the mental and economic imperialism of present times. Through discussions and discourse, the lamp of Rama's name can be lighted in the threshold of every human heart; as said by poet Tulsidas–

"Raam naam mani deep dharu, jeeha dehri dwar,
Tulsi bheetar baahirhun, jo chahasi ujiyaar"

This book is a collection of articles inspired by these feelings. Actually, The Department of Hindi, Tezpur University, Tezpur, Assam had organized a three day International Conference in November, 2017 on the topic "Rama in Asian Life, Literature and Art (In special context of North East India)" in collaboration with Ayodhya Research Institute, Ayodhya, Department of Culture, Government of Uttar Pradesh and Vani Foundation, New Delhi. It was a matter of pride that scholars and participants from inside and outside the country, participated in the conference, organized in this beautiful area of North East India. It is an evidence of the presence of Rama in the global life, literature and art. This book is the collection of the keynotes of the speakers and selected articles, presented by the participants in the conference. Most of the selected articles are related to the 'Assamese Ramkatha' and some others are related to the Ramkatha of the other states of North East India as well as from outside the country, especially from Sri Lanka and Thailand. All these articles have their own importance, in order to understand the relevance of Ram katha in a wider perspective at the global level.

In this collection there are total eighteen articles of different flavors. It means there is diversity in the selected articles in terms of text and texture, both. I believe that readers will like this diversity and definitely appreciate it.

The subject matter of the articles are almost same as the writers have submitted. I have not touched that and tried to present them as original as they are. It is not necessary to say that the responsibility of the originality of the selected articles of this collection is upon their authors. My consent is not compulsory with the views and opinions of the authors. Actually, disagreement has more value in the system of democracy.

Offering indebtedness is just a formality but it is essential for self-satisfaction. Therefore, in this sequence first of all I pay my heartiest thanks to Ayodhya Research Institute, Ayodhya, and its respected and energetic director Dr. Yogendra Pratap Singh, who has provided full financial support for organizing the conference and also given the permission for the publication of this book under the glorious scheme of 'Ramkatha in Indian Languages' of the Institute. He has always inspired me for the hard research work in this field. I will remain grateful for his great, efficient and experienced direction. I offer my sincere thanks to the publisher of this book, Shri Arun Maheshwari, Managing Director, Vani Publication, Delhi and the Chairman of Vani Foundation, Delhi for his co-operation and every possible support in the organization of the conference and the publication of the book. Actually, Mr. Maheshwari is not only the publisher of this book, but is also the Sutradhara of this entire academic activity. Today, this book is able to come in front of you in a physical form only because of his precious suggestions and consultations. At the end I would like to offer my heartfelt and sincere gratitude to my father, Prof. Shivmangal Rai, who has/had always been my academic icon and source of inspiration. I remember the love and affection of my mother, wife and daughter that has always energized me during this complete academic journey and developed an interest towards the accomplishment of this duty. I have no words to offer thankfulness to my students, without whose co-operation, the success of this academic project would have been impossible.

If this collection gets some popularity or success among the readers, the whole credit would go to the contributors or authors of the articles compiled in the book. Now the book is infront of you. Your responses and suggestions are awaited.

Anushabda
Assistant Professor
Department of Hindi
Tezpur University, Tezpur
Assam-784028
anush@tezu.ernet.in/anushabda@gmail.com

CONTENTS

Chapter I

Ramayana, Ram Story and Nuptial Songs : Re-telling of Ram Story in the Context of Assamese Oral Literature

Dr. Juri Gogoi Konwar

The epic "Ramayana" is considered as one of the important mythological texts in Indian literature and culture. The Ramayana stories are perennial favourite and have percolated down to almost all the communities of India. Throughout India there are many variations and versions of the stories. Every community have their own version of Ramayana.

The poet Valmiki, first wrote Ramayana down 2000 years ago. The Ramayana has spread to too many Asian countries. The religions of Buddhism, the Ramayana and related literatures, were carried to Southeast Asia by merchants and pilgrims. The story became embedded into the life and culture of Southeast Asian peoples, and they created their own versions that reflected their own social aspirations and ideological concerns. There are literally hundreds of versions of the story of Rama in India alone, not to mention versions in Thailand, Malaysia, Cambodia, Laos, Indonesia etc. Each version takes a different approach to embroidering the basic narrative and characters. For example, in India, Thailand, Indonesia, and Cambodia, royalty associated themselves with Rama and looked on him as ideal. In South Asia, Sri Lanka, demons become noble and heroic (may be the Lanka of the epic). In Bali, Rama is considered an important person. In India, he is worshipped as an actual god. The Rama story – known as Rama Zatdaw in Burmese (Myanmar) – continued to be transmitted orally from generation to generation up till the 16th century. Hikayat Seri Rama, the Malay version of the epic poem, gives Lakshmana a larger role and even increases his importance as compared to Rama in some incidents. In Thai version most, of the stories are the same as those in Valmiki's version, but Ramakien gives more importance to Hanuman. The Indonesian Ramayana, Kakawin Ramayana differs markedly from the original Hindu prototype. The first half of this Ramayana, Jawa is similar to the original Sanskrit version, while the latter half is divergent to the point of being unrecognizable by Indian scholars of the original Ramayana. In Indian Ramayana portrays Sita as a soft and beautiful woman whereas Indonesian Ramayana depicts her as bold, strong and powerful. She fights with Asuras and Asuris in Sri Lanka herself, without depending on her husband for her freedom from Ravana's ten thousand wives. Phra Lak Phra Lam is the national epic of the Lao people, and is adapted from Valmiki's epic, the Ramayana. Ramayana reached Laos much later than Cambodia and Thailand (Siam) which caused the loss of its original Hindu influence and affected local adaptation. In the Reamker, Cambodian Ramayan, issues of trust, loyalty, love, and revenge are played out in dramatic encounters between princes and giants, monkeys and mermaids, and a forlorn princess.

Among the communities of Northeast India oral tradition of Ramayana appears to be highly rich and colourful. The Mizo have a tale 'Khena- Ramate Unao Thawnthu', apparently influenced by the Ramayana in which a seven-headed Ravana figures. Rama Katha forms an integral part of the culture of Manipur. Rama worship have been patronized by King Ghairb Niwaz, (Pamheiber C 1709-1749) who is credited with the building of the Ramji and Hanumanji temples in Manipur (Dodiya, 2001).

Ramayana has many forms and many different texts both literary and oral. The earliest version of the Assamese Ramayana is the 14th century work of Madhava Kandali which is a compact and faithful adaption from the Valmiki Ramayana. The story of Ramayana travelled beyond borders and became indigenous with various elements of the episodes that match with the local cultural ethos. It is significant that the manuscript of a Buddhistic version of the Ramayana is found among the holy scriptures of a number of small tribal communities of this region (North East India) who practice form of Hinayana Buddhism of Burmese affiliation (Dutta 1999). He also stated that all the tribes are more or less well acquainted with the stories and characters of the great Indian epics, particularly of the Ramayana. In fact many stories of the epics either in their original form or with certain local twist are popular among the tribal groups. The Ramayana story has been a perennial favorite and it has percolated down to almost all the communities of North East India including Assam. Oral tradition of Ramayana in North East India appears to be highly rich and colourful. Ramayana finds many expressions in the folk literatures of Assam and the stories related to Rama has been integrated with the Assamese society. Frequent references of Rama, Sita, Lakshman and other characters of Ramayana have been found in everyday life of the people.

In Assam, the Karbis, they have Karbi version of Ramayana as Sabin Alun with more than one variant. There are Khamti version of Ramayana. The Khamti Ramayana Cao-alang- Lamang, is mostly with the story of Rama's Incarnation. The Phakes, the Khamyangs, the Aitons, the Turungs have kept alive the tradition of Rama Katha since long past. The Tiwas also have their version of Ramayana story which is not a systematically arranged version, since it was orally transmitted.

In Assamese society, Ramayana flourished towards the end of 14th century A.D due to the poet Madhav Kandali. He rendered Valmiki's Ramayana into Assamese verses. From his composition the Ramayana appeared in varied forms- in verses, prose and in songs. After this Ramayana finds many expressions in the folk literatures of Assam and the stories related to Rama have been integrated with the Assamese. The Assamese language is fairly rich in Ramayana lore of both literary and oral traditional affiliations. A whole lot of traditional and folk media like the bhaona, the ojapali (biyah goa/Ramayana goa variety), the bhari gaan and the puppet, theatre has been at work in handling down and disseminating the Ramayana lore.

Gradually with time the stories and more particularly the characters such as Rama, Sita and Laxman were frequently referred in everyday life of people. They were found to be used in day to day practice in the form of proverbs, idioms, incantations, songs and normative behaviour.

Example of proverb- Ram u nai hei ayodhya u nai- used to connote to no existence of whatever is being expected to be.

Example of normative behaviour- Ram ram ki korili – Ram Ram What have you done!

Ram Tangun (Stick), Ram tengor (claver) Ram thogon (Cheated) etc. "Ram" is used here to mean the greatness of something, more in amount.

There is another example of a folk song which is generally sung on the day of Kati Bihu, (one of the festival of Assamese people). This bihu is celebrated in the evening time by illuminating lamps in front of Tuloshi plant (Basil) and paddy field. The song goes like- Tuloxir tole Mrigapohu Sore, Take dekhi Ramchandrae hara dhenu dhare. And the people used to relate the marks of the moon as tuloshi plant and mrigo pahu or the golden deer.

Likewise the reference of Ram-Sita as an ideal couple is very much used in the context of marriage in Assamese society. Marriage is an important social institution of uniting man and woman through familial bonding, proclaiming them to be husband and wife for the very cause of maintaining progenies. This solemn function is celebrated through song, dance and food. Nuptial or Marriage songs can be considered as significant oral literature of Assam. These songs are called as 'biyanam' in vernacular and has the full description of 'Rama and Sita' with poetic creations which are considered to be sacred. Singing of biyanams during the marriage ceremony creates a sacred environment. The songs recount the great wedding of 'Sita and Rama' portraying groom to be Rama and bride as Sita. In a traditional Assamese marriage, various rituals are performed during the whole celebration. On such occasion womenfolk sing different nuptial songs (biyanams) through which they advise, wish and bless the bride as well as the groom for having an ideal conjugal life like that of Rama and Sita. The paper throws some light on how the rich oral tradition of Assamese literature has preserved the devotional elements of Ramayana rature.

The Assamese marriage has many stages and every stages contain various rituals. The significance of every ritual is enhanced by singing the biyanaam. The songs are sung by women in the gathering for marriage ceremony where the men do not usually enter. They constitute a fairly connected story or character of the epic Ramayana. Different biyanaam are there for different rituals. The reference of 'Ram" in the biyanaam are sung particularly during the rituals of Jurun, ceremonial fetching of water for bathing and welcoming the groom where the importance of the groom in her life is made realise to the bride. The sacredness is intact in the ritual through the use of dhup, dhuna, saki, banana leaves etc. as devotional element to welcome the groom (lord Rama).

Burn dhup (insence stick)
The jurun has come
Let's go and welcome them.

The society construct the Rama story in a marriage ceremony mostly with the nuptial songs. Re-telling of Rama story twining with marriage is seen in an Assamese marriage. In a traditional Assamese marriage, various rituals are performed during the whole celebration but in every ritual, marriage songs are not sung mentioning Rama and Sita.

Jurun is one function which takes place at bride's house prior to main marriage ceremony. The journey starts from the groom's house to the bride's place. All along the way womenfolk sing Biyanaam (nuptial songs). Once they reach the bride's house the groom's mother is welcomed by the bride's mother at the very entrance of their place with Sarai containing betal nut and leaves covered by a Gamosa. Earthen lamps and incense sticks are lighted on this occasion, which creates a heavenly ambience. The groom's mother offer the bride ornaments, traditional bridal trousseau along with betel nut, coconut, fish etc. which are the symbols of prosperity and fertility. These Jurun songs sung in Jurun ritual are partly celebratory and partly melancholic.

Some of the biyanaam of the rituals are as follows-

After the arrival of Groom's mother for Jurun ceremony, the woman folk sings –

Ram's mother has arrived,
and she is waiting,
in the door step,
under the welcome gate of banana sapling,
along with the box of presentation for the bride.
Or they sing like....
Koikeyi, Koushlya both of them are coming, o Ram
Give the information to aidew (bride)
Call all the relatives of paternal and maternal line, o Ram
Welcome the tekeli (box of gifts)
****
Keep away the jewelry given by your mother
Keep away the jewelry given by your father
Rama is sending
Beautiful jewelry
Accept it with folded hand
****
Please put vermillion, o
Put vermillion
By taking the pointer (xola)
You are the first daughter-in-law
of King Dasaratha
****
Sage Viswamitra asked for Ram, o hari
To save Tapuban
He saved Tapuban, killed demon Taraka
And broke Hara's bow (Haradhanu)
After breaking the haradhanu, he sat in the royal court
So that no one can marry Sita.
Ram's mother is in Ayoudhya, o hari
He sends the message to her
After getting the news Koushalya came, o hari
Along with vermillion (symbol of married women)
Packing a pure vermillion called Kam sendur
and a pointer (xola)
Bringing folded silk mekhela, o hari

And blouse
Riha is of dotted motif (buta bosa) in two ends
Chadar is of golden brocade with colour in between (bon kora)
For neck she is bringing golden necklace (Xatxori), o hari
For hand bangles
For ear golden earing (lokaparo)
For arm armlet (baju)
For ten fingers ten rings
For leg anklet (nupur)
Bride is beautifying with Ram's jewelry,
All invitees are looking at Sita, surrounding her
Sita is so beautiful that no one will find this beauty anywhere.

From the nuptial songs it is clearly understood that the oral tradition of Assamese literature has preserved the devotional elements of Ramayana and this is likely to sustain in the marriage and other associated rituals in Assamese culture and tradition. There are many more biyanaam sung by the Assamese women mentioning Rama. In Ramayana, Sita is portrayed as beautiful, devoted to Rama and acts as a loving and responsible mother. She is unselfish and self-sacrificing. Subtle expression of patriarchy was through legends, folk songs highlighting the self-sacrificing, self-effacing pure image of women are observed in Ramayana story. Sally Sutherland also speaks about how — The duties of these ideal role models are divided according to their gender; a man's primary concern is his dharma, while a woman's is her husband (http://shodhganga.inflibnet.ac.in/bitstream/10603/90036/10/10_chapter_04.pdf). As the Ramayana stories are based on patriarchal notions, considering the groom as Rama (God) and the bride as Sita, the sacred entity is brought into the particular rituals where it connotes that the bride should from that moment consider or accept the groom as her lord and devote her life to him, as Sita did to Rama in Ramayana. Women began to internalize this patriarchal norms which is culturally imposed and socially constructed.

Reference

1. Dodiya, J. 2001: Critical Perspectives on the Ramayana, Swarup and Sons, New Delhi
2. Dutta B. 1999: Folkloric Foraging in India's North East, ABILAC, Guwahati
3. http://shodhganga.inflibnet.ac.in/bitstream/10603/90036/10/10_chapter_04.pdf

ऋषि भारद्वाज

Chapter II

Sinta Kungri and The Somahadi

(In Search of Sita and Suparnakha through Sabin Alun, the Karbi oral narration of Ramayana)

Dr. Moushumi Kandali

The diversity of the narrative tradition of Ramayana unfolds through Revisiting, Refashioning, Re-appropriating and Retelling of the original text in various literary cultures of India. This article is an attempt to bring to light one such Retelling and Re-appropriation in form of an oral rendition called Sabin Alun by one of the indigenous tribes of Assam, the Karbis, by taking into account the representational aspects of both literary and the visual culture. Sabin Alun, the Karbi Ramayan is the only one of its kind in Assam to elucidate with shared sensibilities and radical difference the tale of Rama in their indigenous cultural setting. Whereas Madhav Kandali's Ramayan (Traceable to 1350s) is a retelling following the original text in terms of location, narration and cultural milieu. Despite certain differences in poetic imagination or style of expression, the karbi oral narration is radically different in terms of its specific ethnic manifestation and indigenous cultural elements and components. In this critical probing, besides reflecting upon the shared troupe and departures from the original Sanskrit text or the mainstream narration, the focus will be given on the poetic representation of Sinta Kungri, which is a subtle refashioning of Valmiki's Sita in Karbi imagination. In doing so, the depiction and characterization of Thesomahadi, the karbi Supranakha will also be brought into deliberation for comparative analysis.

Mainly three sources formulate the premise of this investigation and research :

1. The Assamese compilation of Sabin Alun by Premkanta Mahanta, who travelled and collected the oral verses from various places in Karbi Anglong. Sri Joysingh Doloi, the then President of Diphu Sahitya Sabha published it in 1976. Writer Jagyeswar Sarma, the President of

the Asom Sahitya inaugurated the copy and gave a talk about the same in the Sahitya Sabha Adhibheshan in Tihu, educating about the great oral tradition in mass popular level.

2. The second compilation and Assamese translation by late Samsingh Hanse, published by Asom Sahitya Sabha in 1986. The most significant feature of this compilation is pictorial illustration by artist Biren Sinha. Though due to some technical error the name of the artist has not been mentioned, but by the artist's testimony, along with other testimonials one can establish the authorship of these pictorial illustration.
3. The vast data base and archival documentation in form of audio video recordings by Dharam Singh Teron, the eminent writer, cultural and political activist and the founder Director of Centre for Karbi Studies, a research organisation based at Diphu, district capital of Karbi Anglong.
4. Others sources include interaction with Karbi resource person and well known author Sri Rong Bong Terang and other bibliographical references of some articles though very limited in number.

The Karbis are one of the major ethnic groups in North-east India and especially in the hill areas of Karbi Anglong district in Assam. In constitution, Karbis are mentioned as Mikirs. They prefer to call themselves Karbi, and sometimes Arleng literally which means "man" in the Karbi language. Mikir is the name given by the other groups of plain people to the residents of the hill areas in between the Naga Hills and Jayantia Hills from Dhansiri river to Kiling river. There is no historical record, archaeological finding, literary sources etc. to locate the origin of Karbi tribes. In the old chronicles and Buranjis occasional references here and there were made to the people of this race. But from these references also it is very difficult to trace the chronological events of the Karbis. Their folk-tales and folk-lores are the only sources from which it can have an idea regarding their early history.

According to some scholar, Karbis trace their origin and existence in China and South-east Asia. The Karbis belong to greater Mongoloid racial stock. Linguistically, they belong to the Tibeto-Burman group. They entered Assam from Central Asia through migration. They were among the first group of people who migrated to this land. Some scholars such as Kalaguru Bishnu Prasad Rabha, a noted cultural doyen who had done extensive studies about the ethnic groups of Assam and their indigenous culture has called the Karbis, the Discoverer of Assam– the 'Columbus ancient Assam.'

The Sabin Alun : The celestial musician as the narrator Lunse

Lunse narrating the Sabin Alun. Art work by artist Biren Sinha.

Valmiki in Popular Pictorial imaginatin and Lunse in pictorial illustration (Detial) By artist Biren Sinha.

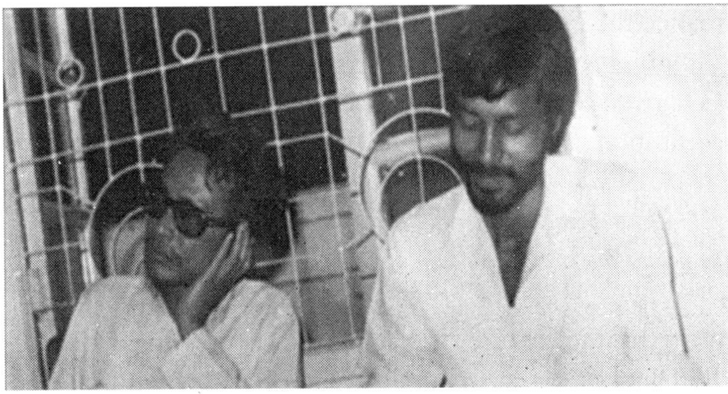

Artist Biren Sinha (Right) with the compiler and translator Late Samsingh Hanse during the time of the project at Diphu in 1986.

The Epic Ramayana has a distinct appeal on the Karbi mind. They have a lengthy tale of almost all the events narrated in Ramayan in form of oral performative narration. The narrator 'Lunse' describes the whole epic in rhythmic musical rendition which can go on for three days. However, there are oral verses which say that originally the first lunsep of Karbi Ramayana, the first composer-performer duo, Chedu and Longbi brothers took twelve days and nights to render the entire epic in the kingdom of Kasen in front of entire community within that locality. The story of Ram, Lokhimon (Lakshman), Sinta Kungri (Sita) and Ulimon (Hanuman) gets appropriated poetically in karbi imagination within their own cultural setting, social fabric, belief system and ritualistic contexts.

In contrast to the original Sanskrit Ramayan of Valmiki, the karbi Ramayan has its own version about the genesis of the epic. As narrated in the beginning episode of the Sabin Alun, the supreme God of the Karbis and the creator of this universe, Hemphu became anxious that the Karbis had till date no music tradition. He called the celestial musician Rangchena and ordered O great musician descend down to the earth and plant the Tree of Music in the Land of the Karbis. Accordingly Rangchena took form of two twin brothers named Mirzeng and came down to dwell on the bank of spring Teleho and started practicing and performing enchanting music. When the festival of Harvest came both of them went to village Abi. Chedu and Longbi, two other brothers of the village welcomed them warmly and purified the sitting space with sacred basil leaves. Then they brought the Horbong, the string instrument and started singing the one thousand sacred verses. They taught these two brothers all the verses and declared them the Lunses, the great musicians and left for the heavenly abode. It was also prescribed that the Lunse would be honoured with ritual at the beginning at and at the ending of the performance the great creator Hemphu should be worshipped. Therefore, Chedu and Logbi, the first Karbi Lunse started travelling all around the Karbi Kingdom. The first performance happened in Kasen, where they addressed the entire community:

Listen to the Sabin Alun, the sacred epic about Ram and Sinta Kungri for twelve days and night. Please bring as offering a cock, rice bear and betel nut and leaf. The cock will be sacrificed and the rice bear would be offered to Great Hemphu who is the source of Sabin Alun.

The most striking feature of Sabin Alun is creating a counter tradition. Complete Retelling in a new cultural setting of their own indigenous cultural milieu with the distinct ethnic flavour of the Karbi brings forth a radical difference from the original narration. Some of the most striking features are as the given in the following :

- The king Janaka of Sabin Alun doesn't plough the land but does jhum or shifting cultivation, a distinct method of indigenous cultivation of the hill people. He sits in the bamboo hut in the field to watch over the paddy fields while drinking wine liquor or rice beer.
- Ram and Lokhimon on their first visit to Janakas Palace sits in the portico of his palace, build on bamboo platform with timber posts and thatch exactly like the house of a village headman. They are offered Horlung,the rice beer and rice.
- Ram, the brave warrior goes out for hunting boar and deer wearing karbi Male apparel.

To be precise, Valmiki's characters appear in reincarnation and emerge in rare depiction in karbi avatar with their religious belief system, social and cultural set up. So eventually the naming changes too : Dasharath become Dorhom, Lakshman Lokhimon, Sita Sinta, Hanuman Ulimon, Parashuram Borpurram, Jatayu Womu Rambepi, Supranakha the Thesomahadi except for Ram, who retains the original name. Moreover, the places also gets appropriated into the Karbi locality or nearby areas of the karbi Anglong hills such as Chitrakut which transforms into Langlung forest. The place called Tezpur is supposed to derive its name from the bloods flowing from the body of Ravana, whose body collapsed here instead of Lanka. In fact, there is a place called Lanka in the district which evokes the resonance of Valmiki's Lanka within the local setting.

The story line and narrational structure also undergo changes with various addition and subtraction, erasure, subversions. Dasharath has only two wives, Janaka is the quintessential farmer, Kaikeyi is perennially absent, Only Ram and

Lokhimon are the two sons of Dorhom. Lokhimon does not marry Urmila and is a bachelor during the exile, Supranakha herself takes the form of a deer, there is a big fight between Ram and Lokhimon after Sinta's abduction. They reconcile only when they eat rice from the same plate and brotherly love resurfaces as a result, Ulimon demand a feast from Ram and Ram cooks Rice and pork with his own hand to feed his dearest bhakta, the spirit of Ravana resides in a bamboo pole in the bedroom of his palace. It is cat dropping which saves Lokhimon's life, not any Sanjivani herb !

Ram breaking the Bow : Sabin Alun illustration by artist Biren Sinha

Laxmana fighting Ravana : Sabin Alun illustration by artist Biren Sinha

Rama fighting Lav Kush : Sabin Alun illustration by artist Biren Sinha

Laxmana on death bed in the battle of Ramayana : Sabin Alun illustration by artist Biren Sinha

Sinta Kungri : The Indigenous Karbi version of Sita's Characterisation

The karbi Sita "Sinta Kungri" is an epitome of the quintessential karbi cultural representation : The ideal Karbi Woman. She exudes physical prowess and deep understanding of indigenous knowledge system and folk belief. Unlike Valmiki's Sita, she is born out of a peacock egg. Sinta's characterisation unfolds multiple attributes:

The Daughter of the farmer and the Forest woman

Sinta clears the forest for jhum cultivation. She cultivates herbal plants in the garden and the courtyards. She, with great physical prowess cuts big trees, lifts them to clear forest like any male counterpart. Herself builds up a counter narrative of the traditional gendered self of the mainstream Indian representation in patriarchy as tender, docile female, subjectivity restricted to the domesticity/interiority of the inner courtyard or the household. As the labour is described with meticulous detail she emerges as a counter imagery reflective of the woman folk from the ethnic groups of north east in general or the karbis in particular. Forest is associated with wilderness and the field with civilization and domestication. Similarly in cultural imagination, wild she is woman, domesticated she is wife as mentioned by Devdutta Pattnaik in the book "In Search of Sita" edited by Malashri Lal and Namita Gokhale. Wherein in case of Sinta kungri, this binary gets erased or transcended as she easily shuffles between the hill woman who frequents the hills and forests to collect things and the domesticated one who clear trees for cultivation. Moreover, she is an expert in making rice beer and cooking meat which she offers to any guest who visits Janaka or takes it to her father who is working in the paddy fields. She crosses serpentine paths and deep forest alone to meet her father who is engaged in jhum cultivation in some faraway hills. She is strong, fearless, brave.

Sinta Kungri of karbi imagination
Picorial illustration by artist Biren Sinha

Sita of mainstream popular cultural imagination
In a calendar at depiction

She Weaves flowers and butterflies in multiple hues : Sinta, the Weaver

There is a beautiful couplet capturing Sinta as a master weaver in Sabin Alun. Of course, this again is a reflective attribute of the Karbi woman who is usually an expert weaver making fine garments in her hand loom. But the poetic imagination further explicate the artistic imagination of Sinta very poignantly. Unlike any other Ramayana, the karbi Sita is seen deeply engaged in weaving during her days in exile.

Under a banyan tree
there is a huge flat rock
near their hut in forest.

Sita sits on that rock weaving
Silk clothes with colourful borders
depicting flowers
and butterflies of multiple hues.

In the realm of visual culture, the agency of the women as an imaginative subject lies in weaving and quilting since other sources of material cultures are not available to her in a patriarchal system unlike her counterpart. However, here medium is not important but her artistic engagement which is of great significance. Despite the fact that it was a gender role that women had to play in a traditional social system, her artistic sensibility gave a meaningful substance to her being though often unacknowledged. The special emphasis on Sinta 's ability as a great imaginative and innovative weaver gives an extra and added dimension to the poetic composition of Sabin Alun.

She proclaims this ought to happen : Sinta as omniscient prescient

Compared to Ram in Karbi imagination who is humanised often rather than being deified, Sinta emerges as the omniscient prescient who knows about the play of the destiny and divine design about the very purpose of the incarnation of Rama and Sinta to establish justice and truth in the world. When Ravana abducts Sinta, Ram and Lokhimon follow like two wild deers across the hills and forest. Upon looking them despaired and lamenting she consoles them :

This ought to happen, it is pre-designed by cosmic forces to reinforce the rule of good over evils. Don't worry, nothing will happen to me.

Thus, Sinta Kungri emerges as more powerful and confident subject as compared to Ram who fails to grasp the divine designs and cosmic intervention and acts like a common mortal, devoid of any divine attribute or qualities of a subject of higher thoughts.

De-deification of Ram or humanization of his character into a common mortal male happens in two other contexts too. At the moment of reunion after the killing of Ravana, Ram forbids Sinta to come near him. He says :

I suspect your chastity Sinta, you have stayed in hostage with another male, so who knows what happened and thou shall give the test of fire.

In another incident when Ram witnessed pregnant Sinta drawing a picture of Ravana on the ground on the insistence of the palace women (She says she never saw Ravana but only his reflection once on the water), Ram screams like a commoner :

You are a witch incarnate. You were in love with Ravana and perhaps the child inside your womb is born out of Ravana's seed.

She leaves the palace at midnight : Sinta, the silent dissenter

Sinta kungri doesn't utter a word when Ram orders for the test of fire or sends her to exile. Sinta who is adequately vocal in the Karbi Ramayana remains staunchly silent.

Why is Sinta silent? She doesn't protest to any such injustice, but remains completely silent. Is it her assertion of independent self, expressed in utter intense grief of being subjected to injustice in extreme form ? As if in culmination of this silent dissent, she, unlike Valmiki's Sita, who takes refuse in mother earth in front of the entire kingdom of Ayodhya, Karbi Sinta walks out of the Ram's palace at midnight in silence when the whole world sleeps. Unlike Valmiki's Sita, who bids farewell to all and allows information to flow, Karbi Sinta Kungri leaves everyone in suspense, she doesn't allow the information to flow, she suppresses it by not letting anyone know because by letting information about oneself we exhibit attachment, or a sense of belonging and bonding. Sinta abandons all making everyone wild in utter ignorance about her whereabouts, about her existence or non existence. She shuns the world making them realize that silence can be louder, evocative and hard hitting than loud pronouncement. Ram and the entire humankind writhe in pain, repentance, remorse and helplessness of ignorance. Sinta crosses many forest many hills as if both reliving and recuperating her entire journey of grief to finally take refuge in mother earth.

Sita's refuge in mother Earth : Sabin Alun illustration by artist Biren Sinha

Sisterhood of Sita and suparnakha: The complete subversion

In a most striking deviation of any Ramayanic narration, The Karbi Sita and Karbi Supranakha Thesomahadi do not emerge as mutual alter egos unlike the mainstream depiction. This is perhaps the high point of Karbi imagination. Sita and Supranakha exemplify two types of women who appears almost universally in folklore and mythology : Sita is good, pure, light, auspicious and subordinate, whereas Supranakha is evil, impure, dark, inauspicious and insubordinate. They appear as alter ego where Sita is chaste, good, ideal woman and Supranakha, the loose bad unbridled woman with un-channelized sexuality.

In karbi Ramayan both the women encounter each other and experience highest kind of mutual appreciation. Both find each other extremely beautiful (Thesomahadi is not in disguise of a beautiful woman as seen in Valmiki Ramayan), cordial, amicable. Sinta expresses her desire to make Thesomahadi her sister-in-law as Lokhimon is still a bachelor. Thesomahadi exudes happy radiance as that was her inner desire too as she fell in love at first sight with Lokhimon because of his physical strength and valour. Sinta gives the proposal to Lokhimon who rejects with utter anger and upon looking at Thesomahadi few days later with Sita he mutilates her. Sinta condemns in sharpest tongue possible for rejecting her love and also for mutilating a woman. The ethno-racial difference between Sinta and Thesomahadi is apparent in the epic narration of Sabin Alun. Thesomahadi has been described as a member of Rakshash, as the sister of Ravana. The pictorial illustration of Sinta and her two Rakshashi attendant in Ashok Vatika in Lanka exemplify the ethno –racial physical attribute of Rakshash female to which Thesomahadi belongs too.

Sita's in Ashok Vatika : Sabin Alun illustration by artist Biren Sinha

Hence, it is really interesting to note that despite the ethno-racial, physical differences and other differences in terms of their nature, the representations of Sinta and Thesomahadi do not emerge as alter ego. Rather a very rare concept of Sisterhood emerges in a very subtle yet significant way by the very act of Sinta's marriage proposal to Thesomahadi, her way of seeking consent and then further taking that proposal to Lokhimon. Sinta's constant attempt at negotiation comes up as a signification for transcending all the binaries between these two characters, despite their ethno-racial, ethno-cultural differences and differences in human-nature and mental make up. This is one of the most radical subversion seen in any Ramayanic depiction so far in this particular context. Reference to the mainstream pictorial depiction of Supranakha's mutilation by Laxmana further substantiate the argument as here Sita is a mute spectator whereas in the literary composition of Sabin Alun, she is not.

Popular depiction of Suparnakha's mutilation : Calendar Art

Sabin Alun : Song of Suparnakha ?

Finally, I would like to draw the attention to the name of the Karbi Ramayan itself. The meaning of Sabin Alun is the Songs of SABIN. There are two probability here : That, it is about the songs by Sabin. Or, that It is song about Sabin. It is herein worth mentioning that Sabin is a female name as authenticated by Karbi scholars like Writer Rongbong Teron and researcher Dharam Singh Teron.

Now a very crucial question arises, WHO IS SABIN ? Is she the actual author of the epic narration, or the Narrator ? A narrator, oral composer who created this vibrant literary tradition with a story about its genesis as the preface?

Or is she a character in the epic narration?

Apparently, there is no character called Sabin in the epic narration.

However, as recorded by Dharam Singh Teron in his audio-visual documentation of Sabin Alun under a project taken by the Centre for Karbi Studies (Based at Diphu, Karbi Anglong), Sabin is another name for Thesomahadi. The oral verbal testimonial of one of the Sabin Alun performers of the oral narration, Kareng Teronpi, who is 76 years old is accountable for this assumption. According to Kareng Teronpi, it is Thesomahadi as Sabin claims in one of the couplets:

It is me for whom the entire phenomenon of Ramayana happened, it is me for whom Ram and Ravan and all other met, I am the cause of all that happened, I led to the establishment of good, so why should not the Epic be named after me ? So let this be known as narration of Sabin- Sabin Alun.

Going by this claim, Sabin Alun is neither Ramayana, nor Sitayana but Supranakhayan! Perhaps, it is the ultimate Subversion of any Ramayanic narration.

Bibliography

1. Richman, Paula. "Questioning Ramayana, A south Asian Tradition ", Oxford University Press, New Delhi.2000.
2. Richman, Paula. "Many Ramayanas, The Diversity of a Narrative Tradition in South Asia. Oxford University Press, New Delhi. 1992.
3. Smith, W. L. "Ramayana Traditions in Eastern India", Munshiram Manoharlal Publishers Pvt. Ltd. New Delhi.1995.
4. Nair, CN. Sreekantan and Sara Joseph. " Retelling Ramayana, Voices from Kerala". Oxford University Press, New Delhi.2005.
5. Lal, Malashri and Namita Gokhale. "In Search of Sita, Revisiting Mythology". Penguin Books, New Delhi.2009.
6. Ghosh, Sujit K. "Epic As History, Diffusion of Ramkatha From Chin Hills to Lushai Hills". B R Publishing Corporation. New Delhi.2011.
7. Bhattacharjee, T. "Sociology of the Karbis." B R Publishing Corporation. New Delhi. 1986.
8. Lyall, Sir Charles. "The Karbis". Spectrum Publications, Delhi. 1997.
9. Das, Basanta. Edited by Ajit Signar. " karbi Sansritir Itihaas". Aank Baak Publishers, Guwahati. 2010.
10. Terang, Rong Bong. "Karbi Sanskritir Ruprekha. Asam Sahitya Sabha. Jorhat.2010.
11. Terang, Rong Bong. "Karbi Sahityor Saurabh. (Part I)" Deputy Directorate Information and Public Relations (Jyotormoy Chakravarty), Karbi Anglong Autonomous Council, Diphu, 2014.
12. Terang, Rong Bong. "Karbi Sahityor Saurabh. (Part II)" Deputy Directorate Information and Public Relations (Jyotormoy Chakravarty), Karbi Anglong Autonomous Council, Diphu, 2016.

Chapter III

Ramakatha in the Wedding Songs of Assamese People of the Brahmaputra Valley

Dr. Ranjan Chakravarty

It is well accepted by scholars that oral tradition becomes the source of all traditions, so also the literary tradition may again turn into an oral tradition. We get different versions of the Ramayana flourished both in the tribal and non-tribal races of Brahmaputra Valley, which are not directly influenced by the Valmiki Ramayana. In oral tradition of Ramayana the folk-songs of the Brahmaputra Valley are having a significant role, as folk culture and oral tradition are inter related. We get the following classification of folk songs scattered in the Brahmaputra valley.

(i) Jhumur songs, (ii) Tusu geets, (iii) Wedding songs or Marriage songs, (iv) Bambol pita geet, (v) Tulsi geet, (vi) Nawaria geet, (vii) Siva siva geet, (viii) Sita baramahi geet, (ix) Oja pali geet, (x) Dhulia geet, (xi) Bihu and Husari geet, (xii) Lokagit etc.

Thus, folk songs include Wedding songs or marriage songs as well. The Wedding songs or marriage songs which are scattered here and there in the Brahmaputra Valley, have a significant role in the marriage ceremony. It is seen that the marriage songs based on the Ramayana invariably change an Assamese Village to Ayodhya or Mithila as the case may be. The mother of a bridegroom could be converted to Kausalya of Ayodhya, and the father to Janaka of ancient Mithila. No one can ignore the importance of these marriage songs in the society. In the present paper, all possible efforts have been made to present a brief study on almost all the Wedding songs or marriage songs circulated in the Brahmaputra valley since time immemorial, by which the stories of Rama are beautifully mirrored in local design.

Key Words : Wedding Songs, Rama, Brahmaputra Valley.

It is well accepted by scholars that oral tradition becomes the source of all traditions, so also the literary tradition may again turn into an oral tradition. We get different versions of the Ramayana flourished both in the tribal and non-tribal races of Brahmaputra Valley, which are not directly influenced by the Valmiki Ramayana. In oral tradition of Ramayana the folk-songs of the Brahmaputra Valley are having a significant role, as folk culture and oral tradition are inter related. We get the following classification of folk songs scattered in the Brahmaputra valley.

(i) Jhumur songs, (ii) Tusu geet, (iii) Marriage songs, (iv) Bambol pita geet, (v) Tulsi geet, (vi) Nawaria geet, (vii) Siva siva geet, (viii) Sita baramahi geet, (ix) Oja pali geet, (x) Dhulia geet, (xi) Bihu and Husari geet, (xii) Lokagit etc.

Thus, folk songs include marriage songs as well. In the present paper, all possible efforts have been made to present a brief study on almost all the marriage songs circulated in the Brahmaputra valley since time immemorial by which the stories of Ramayana are beautifully mirrored in local design.

Marriage in an important part of human life. It can be defined as a socially sectioned/sanctioned sex relationship involving two or more people of the opposite sex, whose relationship is expected to endure beyond the time required for gestation and the birth of children. This marriage ceremony includes the observances of various rites. Every ritual according to the nature of a marriage ceremony bears some suitable songs known as Biya Nam or Biya geet i.e. marriage songs. The Ramayana plays a vital role in this regard. When a marriage ceremony is held, the bride groom is considered as Rama and the bride as Sita.

The women folk or Ayati's of the Brahmaputra Valley depict their feelings, experiences and traditional beliefs through these marriage songs, which are orally transmitted from generation to generation and have been an integral part of the society. By the marriage songs, the Ramayana is brought down to the level of the life of the common people and the names of Rama and Sita, Dasaratha and Janaka are attributed to the common people. The marriage songs posses a kind of spiritual significance and also blessings to the marital life of the couple. These songs are sung simultaneously with different rituals of the marriage.

At the very beginning the women folk or the Ayati's take permission for singing marriage songs by praying Raghupati :

"O Rama, allow us to sing biya nam or marriage songs". (1)

The confirmation of a marriage ceremony by ceremonial gifts (Juroon) consisting of clothes, ornaments etc. sent for the bride from the bridegrooms house, forms a marriage ritual on which occasion relevant song related to Ramayana is thus sung :

'The Princes wrote a letter on a betal leaf wrote a letter on a betal leaf. Receiving that letter Ramachandra has sent these ornaments. Keep aside the ornaments of your mother, also the ornaments of your father. Rama has sent the variegated ornaments. Take them with folded hands. O Sita, mother of Rama has arrived at. Come out being bow down. Variegated ornaments have been brought in the ceremonial present. Take them bending down your head. Kaikeyi has come, Sumitra has come, the mother of Rama also has come. How charming Janaki, daughter of Janaka, will be decorated today with ceremonial presents, let us see.' (2)

After the Juroon, the next day is the marriage-ceremony. Here, we find two types of marriage songs. (1) Marriage songs, which are sung in the bride-grooms house and

(2) Marriage songs, which are sung in the bride's house.

In various events we find different marriage songs in both-side.

Thus, we find the following classifications of marriage-songs :

(i) Song of bringing water,
(ii) Song of bathing,
(iii) Song of dressing,
(iv) Song of wearing ornaments,
(v) Song of welcoming the bride-groom,
(vi) Song near the Sacred fire,
(vii) Song of bride's weeping,
(viii) Song of fare-wel of the bride,
(ix) Nindageet or jocking songs etc.

We get ample examples of these marriage songs deleneating Rama-Stories. Some of them are given below:

The following marriage song is sung by the women folk of the bride's side, when they go to bring holy water—

— "Come out bride's mother taking water pot in your hand, to bring water from Yamuna river, to give bath to Sita." (3)

In the bride groom's side also the following song is sung at the time of bringing holy water—

— "O, Ram-Krishna, Kausalya is bringing water, donot see backwards, ocean also will be following. O, Ram-Krishna, today in Rama's house, there is a sacrifice or jagita; water is brought from Yamuna" (4).

At the time of bathing we get the following song—

— "Nal-grasses are bending down in the back-side of Sita's (or Ramachandra's) residence.

Planty of water, brought from Yamuna river is poured down for her (or his) bath." (5)

At the evening time after taking bath, both the bride and the bride-groom have to seat in the midst of the women folk for dressing, painting etc. in their own houses. Then the Ayati's sing like following :—

— 'After seating in the Pati (Carpet) Sita fainted, today Mithila city will become dark, and the Ayodhya city will become more bright." (6)

Again —

'Will you have tea-sweets in Janaka's house?

Haradhanu is there, will you have tea-sweets?

Rama is getting very much tension, will you have tea-sweets?

Oh Rama, are you really going (there) to marry?' (7)

When the bride-groom starts his journey towards the bride's home the following song is thus sung:—

"After playing the dhol (a kind of music instrument) Ramachandra starts his journey bowing down to his father." (8)

When the bride-groom reaches the main entrance of the bride's home the Ayati's or the women folk sing :—

"Ramachandra has come, all the mangal badya are played, and beg for Sita at the entrance of the house of King Janaka. Come inside, dear, come; and seat in the Rabhatala; making the sacrificial fire as witness and accept Sita'. (9)

Again we get—

"From Ayodhya Sri Rama has come for the purpose of Sayambara (Marriage) of Janaki (or Sita) " (10).

Then the Ayati's sing the following song :—

"Go, dear lady, go; go near the sacrificial fire and give the garland of the Tagar-flower in the head of Rama." (11)

When the bridegroom walk around the bride the following marriage song is thus sung :—

"What kind of honey is there in the 'Achal' of Sita, looking that Ramachandra is roaming behind Sita." (12)

Again—

"Like ugha, Chereki (instrument of loom); Sita is walking around Rama taking garland in her hand." (13)

After that there is a tradition of hiding ring or playing "Pasha" (gamble) by the bride-groom and the bride.

The relevant song is thus—

"Rama and Sita is gambling, when all the people are looking. If Ramachandra is defeated, what will happen?" (14)

At the last moment when the bride is about to leave her parents home, or at the depurture time of the bride to the bridegroom's house, the women folk sing as follows :—

"Sita is leaving the residence, where she is born and brought up. Today Ramachandra take her away." (15)

In the following marriage song we get a description of Khatara Temple (a very old temple in Darrang Dist., Assam) which is related with Rama Katha—

"O Ram, Khatara Temple, Strange-looking, have 120 pillars. On the front side pictures of Rama and Laksmana is painted. On the other side we see the picture of Sita." (16)

In the marriage ceremonies of the Brahmaputra Valley we find a tradition of Nindagit (or jock-songs) in the marriage songs. As for example :—

"........................., the seating style of the bridegroom is resembled with Hanumana." (17)

— ".... The girls of the bride's-side are told to be from the race of 'Surpanakha." (18)

Among the people of the Tibeto-Burman stock, the Bodos keep the Ramayana tradition alive in their marriage songs. They worship bathau-Sibrai. This God may be equated with Siva. The Bodos are not opposed to other Gods of the Hindus. Hence, the name of Rama and others are found in some folk songs current among them. They believe that narration of the Rama Nama as well as seeing a bride groom in procession are pious deeds. For example :

"Turning to the bride they exhort her,
O sister dear,
Utter the name of the lord Ram
Heart and soul
He alone is the ultimate resort
Rama is the Lord
Death is sure of living beings
You too must die one day
Pray to Rama then
Brothers and sisters and relatives
None is as near as Rama
Virtue and good things done,
Alone will stand by you.
Nothing but these would last." (19)

Thus, it is seen that the marriage songs based on the Ramayana invariably change an Assamese Village to Ayodhya or Mithila as the case may be. The mother of a bridegroom could be converted to Kausalya of Ayodhya, and the father of the Janaka of ancient Mithila. The above songs may be taken as typical example in this regard. Thus we find that the marriage songs which are scattered here and there in the Brahmaputra Valley have a significant role in the marriage ceremony. No one can ignore the importance of these marriage songs in the society.

References

1. O Raghupati biyanam gabalai dia anumati/
2. Panat patra lekhi diyahe aideu
   Panat patra lekhi dila/
   Sei patra khani paye ramachandrai Alankar pathiai dila//
   Marar alankar thowa kati kari Baperar alankar thowa/
   Rame di pathaiche bichitra alankar Hate jure kari lua.//
   Ramera janani palehi rukuni Olai aha mur dowai./
   Junonat aniche bichitra alankar Luahi matha dowai//
   Kaikayi ahiche sumitra ahiche Ahiche ramera mao/
   Janakar jiari janaki sundari Juron pindhua aji cau. //
3. Olai aha Kainar mayek, hate ghata lai, hate ghata lai/
   Yamunare pani ano Sitak dhuwabalai //
4. Ram Krisna jal bhari Kausalya/
   Ram Krisna pachalai nachaba/
   Hari mor ai, Sagar ahiba bhahi//
   Ram Krisna aji Ramar ghare/
   Ram Krisna Kiba Yajna Kare/
   Hari Mor ai anaiche yamunar pani//
5. Sita aideur barir pichat (or Ramachandrar barir pichat)/
   hali ache nal/
   Kalahe kalahe dhale yamunare jal//
6. Patite bohiye O man tagar/]
   Sita murcha gale O man tagar//
   Aji Suda haba Mithila Nagar/
   Ujali uthiba Ayodhya Nagar //
7. Janakar gharate, Chah mithai Khabane?
   Ache Haradhanu chah mithai khabane?
   Ramar mane bara chintahe, chah mithai khabane?
   Sachakai Ram tumi biya haba jabane?
8. Ram Ram dholat kobe mari/
   Ram Ram olal Siri Rama/
   Hari mor ai deutakak namaskar kari//
9. Ramachandra ahiche mangal badya bajaiche/

Janak Rajar padulit Kanya bhiksa magiche//
Jowa bopa jowagai, rabhatalit bahagai/
Homar juik Saksi kari, Sitak grahan karagai //

10. Ram Ram Ajodhyar para/
Ram Ram Sri-Rama ahiche/
Ram Ram janakir Sayambar bulihe//
11. Jowa aideu jowagai, homar guri powagai,
Tagar phular maladhari, Ramar murat diyagai//
12. Sita ayir achalate kiba madhu ache,
Take dekhi Ramachandrai ghure pache pache//
13. Ugha ghure jenekai, chereki ghure tenekai,
Ramar kasat Sita ghure, hate puspa mala lai //
14. Ram Sitai Pasha Khele Raije beri chai,
Ramachandra hare jadi ki haba upay //
15. Tuli tali dangar kara ghar eri jay/
Aji Rame ahi Sitak hari lai jay //
16. Ram Ram Khatara gasaighar/
Ram Ram dekhante bhayankar/
Hari mor O Chakuri naharar khuta//Ram Ram ag-phale likhile/
Ram Ram Rame-Laksmane/Hari mor O' Pich-phale likhile Sita //
17. Eroplanar pailot Eroplanar pailot
Darajan bahi ache Hanumanar Stailat//
18. Ahom Raja gadadhar
Kainagharar Chowali Kaijani Surpanakhar Bansadhar//
19. Ram bun namathi mona zothun cothi ram ram
ram buna bola mona ala zala ram ram/
thoinangon zekhalimona alizali ram ram
bida phonbay ay-apha raobo anni nona/
khulaybo thalangon phop
phuinobo thanphagon ram ram //

Chapter IV

"Ram is a good boy"

Sarat Kr. Doley

Writers of instructional English grammar books or teachers of English as a Second Language (L2) in India often use the name 'Ram' as the subject of an English example sentence. This paper is broadly on the perception of this name. The focus of the paper, however, is not on the grammarians' or teachers' use of the name 'Ram' in grammar lessons. To be precise, it is an attempt mainly at an understanding of a contemporary cultural perception, among the youths, of a traditionally important cultural item, the name 'Ram', through the cognitivist approach. Since the cognitivist approach to cultural discourse considers discourse as a window onto underlying mental processes of the participants involved, the cultural discourses, engaged in by the participants, as a reflection of the underlying mental processes in turn become the bedrock for psychological investigation. Using the responses to a questionnaire on the use of the name 'Ram' as the subject of an example sentence in English Grammar lessons in a study undertaken at Tezpur University, it attempts in general at an analysis of the familiarity and popularity of the term 'Ram' among the youths of Assam.

It, however, relies on two assumptions. First, the use of this name as the subject of an example sentence in English grammar lessons both in the classroom and in study materials on English grammar is assumed by the author as widespread across the state, even though there is no serious study on the subject as yet. Second, it was also assumed at the start of this study that the name 'Ram', though used by the grammarians and the teachers in the context of English as L2 learning, often refers to or has the potential to refer to Ram of the Ramayana.

Despite the very potential situation that both these two assumptions get proven wrong, the assumption that the name 'Ram' is both a familiar and a loaded term in the context of Assam should, though heuristic, would be accepted in principle. The paper attempts in particular at a description and analysis of the English L2 learners' response to the name 'Ram' as and when used in the context of English grammar lessons, relying heavily on the veracity of this assumption. The author believes that the results of this study have the potential to enable significant contemporary understanding about the familiarity and popularity of the name 'Ram' among the youths of the state as well as the country.

The study was carried out at the Department of English and Foreign Languages of Tezpur University, a central university established in the North East Indian state of Assam in 1994. There were a couple of undergraduate programs offered by the department of English and Foreign Languages and the students who took part in this study were students of these two programs: Integrated MA and Integrated BA B.Ed. in English. The biggest limitation of this study is that it did not include the students studying in the undergraduate programs offered by the other schools of the university- School of Engineering, School of Management, and School of Sciences. The reason for the exclusion of the students of these programs was that the questionnaire used as the main tool of the study was related to English language classes. It was suspected that the tool might not be able to extract relevant responses from the student respondents of these programs as the English grammar lessons were either not taught to them or if they were taught to them, the lessons were perceived by them as secondary.

One more reason, perhaps the most important reason, for the exclusion of the students of the School of Engineering, where some grammar lessons were given, was that a pilot study involving them had been conducted on the same issue using the same tool, but because of the immense diversity of the student respondents in terms of geographical origins, since the students were from across the country, the responses were difficult to measure. The responses showed more of a sketchy pan-Indian picture than anything. The pan-Indian picture showed by the pilot study was sketchy because of the fact that, the study was significantly limited by the small size and restricted distribution of the sample, ill-equipped for a study that involved by default a wide coverage. In addition, female representation in the Engineering programs was significantly limited as the ratio of female students against male students in these programs was around 1:25.

It was concluded that the characteristics of these students and the nature of the courses they were studying might not be comparable as the academic situation of the students of Integrated MA and BA B.Ed. in English would necessarily be different from the academic situation of the undergraduate students of the

School of Engineering. It was apprehended that these two different varieties of sample might lead to different unrelated findings. A comparative study involving these two groups of students would be a better approach to the situation, but it was outside the basic objective of the present study.

The undergraduate students of Integrated MA and BA B.Ed. in English, compared to the students of the undergraduate Engineering programs, were more geographically restricted as almost all of them were from the state of Assam. They came from different parts of the state, they belonged to different communities of the state, they were of the same age group, unlike the Engineering courses, and they were also a fairly representative group in terms of sex. The students were enrolled in these programs only after they had completed their higher secondary education or class XII level education, where English grammar lessons were a part of their English language education. The age of the students enrolled in these programs ranged between 18 to 20 years. These students had at least around 5 years of primary, 5 years of high school, and 2 years of higher secondary level education by the time they enrolled for the undergraduate programs at Tezpur University. It was also observed, though not immediately relevant to the study, that a good majority of the students enrolled in these integrated programs came from English medium schools.

The total number of students who participated in the study was 90 and it included all the three semesters of these two integrated programs. The responses from these students were taken in the Autumn semester of 2017. The students represented a fairly accurate demographic situation in the state of Assam excluding the sexual representation where female representation was around double to that of male representation. Since the admission policy of the university was guided by the policy implemented by the government, the sample might be more or less considered a miniature picture of the actual demographic situation in the state. In addition to the division of the students in to units of male and female, they were also grouped into smaller units such as urban/rural, general caste/OBC/SC/ST, and Hindu/others. The percentage of representation of these various units of the sample was as shown in Figure 1 below–

Male – 33.3%	Female-66.6%
Urban- 70%	Rural-30%
General-50%	OBC/MOBC- 26.6%
ST-10%	SC-13.3%
Hindu- 83.3%	Others-16.6%

Figure 1 : Distribution of the sample

Majority of the student respondents were female as the number of female student enrollment in these two programs was relatively higher than male student enrollment. The percentage of female representation was 66.6% and it was twice the percentage of male representation of 33.3%. Although the difference was high in favour of female representation, the male representation was not negligible. The gap was at least not as strikingly wide as it was in the undergraduate Engineering programs. Looking at the subject of the study, this mild gap between the male and the female student representation was not considered capable of significantly affecting the results of the study. The difference between the urban and the rural students was a bit similar to the difference between male and female student representation. The percentage of urban students was around 70% and it was a little more than twice the percentage of rural student of 30%. It was presumed that this difference should also not affect the results of this study exponentially as the rural student representation was also quite high.

The percentage of representation of the students in terms of their communities, almost more or less, matched the demographic, as stated elsewhere, situation in the state. The general caste was represented by 50% of the students, the other backward classes (OBC/MOBC) 26.6%, scheduled tribes (ST) 10%, and the scheduled caste (SC) 13.3%. The representation in terms of religion also showed, more or less, a coincidentally similar picture as the Hindu representation in the sample was 83.3% and the representation of the other religions was 16.6%. The distribution of the sample in relation to the communal characteristics was more important for the present study than the distribution of the sample in terms of place of residence. The communal features of the student respondents had more significant probability of influencing their responses than the other features. More than the other criteria in the list, this important aspect of the sample was emphasized upon in the selection of the sample with the belief that the findings of the study would be a fairly accurate representative picture of the question in hand.

The first item in the questionnaire distributed to the student respondents in the class was related to their familiarity with the name 'Ram'. The student respondents were given two choices and they had to respond to the item either positively or negatively. Quite expectedly, all the student respondents said that they were familiar with the name 'Ram' as the percentage of positive response was 100%. The second item in the questionnaire was related to the first item as it was also associated with their familiarity with the name 'Ram'. But the second item was concerned with the specificity of their knowledge as it asked whether their familiarity with the name of Ram, if they were familiar, had specific identification source. They were given four choices to pick from. The first choice was whether they were familiar with the name 'Ram' as the name of a real life individual, the second whether as a mythological character, the third as a Hindu god, and the fourth offered an option to prefer an identification source not included in the preceding three choices. The percentage of the choices made by the student respondents was as in Figure 2 below-

Only as a name of a real life individual—6.6%
As a mythological character – 80%
As a Hindu god –6.6%
Others (please specify)—6.6%

Figure 2 : Identification Source

As Figure 2 shows, majority of the students knew the name 'Ram' as a mythological character. The percentage of identification choice for this option was 80%. The significant aspect of the responses to this item was that the percentages of the other three options were almost equal as they were hovering at around 6.6%. It was surprising to see that a thumping majority of the student respondents chose the second option where a more popular option, the option that clearly stated 'Ram' as a Hindu god, was available. The student respondents identified the name 'Ram' more with mythologies and legends than with more distinctly perceptive religious sentiments.

The third item in the questionnaire was related to connotative associations triggered by the name 'Ram'. The student respondents were given two choices to pick from. The respondents might either associate the name 'Ram' with positive values or with negative values. Quite expectedly again, the responses were decisively in favour of positive values. All the student respondents, as the percentage of positive value association was 100%, said that they associated the name 'Ram' with positive values. It would be interesting to see the exact and elaborate pool of these positive values associated the name 'Ram', but that was beyond the scope of the present study. But the responses to the fourth item in the questionnaire were unexpected. The fourth item in the questionnaire was related to the appreciation or otherwise of the name 'Ram' when it was used as the subject of an example sentence in an English grammar lesson. Figure 3 below shows the percentage of the choices made by the student respondents-

Like—16.6%
Dislike—6.6%
Indifferent—76.6%

Figure 3 : Student appreciation

Considering the fact that all the student respondents associated the name 'Ram' with positive values, it was expected that the first choice in response to the fourth item would be majority choice. But the least expected choice, the third choice, received a decisive response of 76.6%. Majority of the student respondents were indifferent to the name Ram when it was used as the subject of an example sentence in an English grammar lesson.

The responses to the fifth item in the questionnaire continued to show the trend seen in the case of the fourth item. The fourth item in the questionnaire was restated in a slightly different manner in the fifth. Instead of appreciation choices, it focused on responses in terms of preferences. The fifth item offered the respondents three choices by asking them to state their preference from the choices of a western name, Ram, and others. Figure 4 below shows the preference pattern of the respondents –

Western name-- 26.6%

Ram—16.6%

Others (please specify)—56.6%

Figure 4 : Preference as a name

As Figure 4 indicates, majority of the students preferred other names as the percentage of preference for the third choice was 56.6%. The significant indication of this preference was the percentage of preference shown for the name 'Ram' which received only 16.6% responses, the lowest among the three options. The percentage of responses for even a western name which was 26.6%, the first choice in the item, was more than the responses in favour of the name 'Ram'.

In order to ascertain whether the responses to the fifth item in the questionnaire were accidental or they actually reflected a general tendency of preference, the next four items in the questionnaire were designed to provide different associations in which the name 'Ram' was presented in proximity with comparable statements. The sixth item in the questionnaire offered a pool of five names along with the name 'Ram' drawn from the fields of popular movie and sports that the students were familiar with as the subject of the example sentences. To provide more options, the item also kept the individual preferences open by providing the respondents a choice of name other than the ones presented in the list of example sentences. The popular names included in the item other than 'Ram' were Brad Pitt, Virat Kohli, Zubeen Garg, and Ranbeer Kapoor. These names were then presented in example sentences that associated with the quality of goodness. Figure 5 below shows the percentage of responses to the different example sentences involving these names—

Brad Pitt was a good man—10%
Virat was a good man—16.6%
Zubeen was a good man—16.6%
Ram was a good man—16.6%
Ranbeer was a good man—3.3%
Others (please specify)—36.6%

Figure 5 : Preference for popular names

The surprising thing about the preferences shown by the respondents was that the percentage of student respondents who said they liked the sentence "Ram was a good man" was only 16.6%. Although it was more than the individual percentages of some example sentences with other names in the list, the lack of preference for the example sentence associated with the quality of goodness with the name 'Ram' as the subject of the sentence was contrary to the initial expectations of the researcher. In fact the combined percentage of the preferred example sentences with names other than 'Ram' was astonishingly high at 83.1%. It clearly showed a refusal or lack of motivation to accrue special association of the quality of goodness with the name 'Ram'.

In the next three items in the questionnaire, the name 'Ram' was presented in different other associative environments. The sixth item presented the name 'Ram' with the names of other gods in the Hindu pantheon--Krishna, Shiva, Ganesha, and Vishnu. An additional option of others was also provided to the respondents in order to delimit the association. Continuing the trend seen in the earlier items related to names, the percentage of students who said they liked the sentence "Ram is a good god" as an example sentence was only 3.3%, which was the lowest. It was far less than the percentage of students who liked similar sentences with the names of the four other Hindu gods mentioned in the list or other probable names. It was a whopping 96.7%. It is significant that the percentage of students who preferred other probable names not in the list was 56.6%, which was more than half of the total responses, compared to the percentage of students who liked the example sentences with the names of Hindu gods as the subject.

In the seventh item, the name 'Ram' was presented as the subject of example sentences along with names of gods that belonged to two other important religions. It also kept the option of others open. None of the student respondents showed preference for the example sentence "Ram is the best". Here also, the percentage of responses in favour of the others option was far greater than the responses to the example sentences with religious names. The percentage of preference for the others option was 93.3%. It may be concluded fairly safely that the student respondents at least did not prefer the name 'Ram' with the quality of goodness in the superlative.

The responses to the eighth item in the questionnaire showed similar trend. In this item, the example sentence "Ram was more honest than anybody else" was compared with the example sentence "Sita was more honest than anybody else". The attribute of honesty was associated with names used as the subject of these example sentences. Here again, the percentage of students who said they liked the example sentence "Ram was more honest than anybody else" was only 16.6% which was far less than the percentage of students who preferred names other than 'Ram' as the subject of such example sentences. The percentage of preference for example sentences with names other than 'Ram' was 83.3%. Surprisingly, the percentage of responses in favour of the example sentence "Sita was more honest than anybody else" was 40% which was almost equal to the 43.3% preference shown for example sentences with names other than 'Ram' or 'Sita' when they were associated with the attribute of honesty.

The preference for the name 'Sita' in the associative environment of the attribute of honesty in the example sentences may provisionally be explained by the fact that the majority of the respondents in the study were female students. This provisional explanation is also inconclusive for the fact that majority of the male student respondents did not associate the name 'Ram' with the attribute of honesty in the degree of comparison. A more elaborate study singularly concentrating on this item may provide more reasonable explanation. But then, whatever may be the actual factor behind such a preference, which could not be concluded from the present study, it was quite conclusive that the name 'Sita' was considered more positively associated with the attribute of honesty than the name 'Ram' by the student respondents of the present study.

The last item in the questionnaire was more direct in nature in comparison with the other items with regard to the understanding of the cognitive and emotive responses of the student respondents. The aim of this item was to know what the student respondents felt about the plight of Ram as the hero of the Ramayana. Figure 6 below shows the percentages of the five responses to the choices provided to the respondents—

You idealize –3.3%
You sympathize—6.6%
You do not idealize—33.3%
You do not sympathize –20%
Others (please specify)—36.6%

Figure 6 : Emotional appraisal

The percentages of the responses to the last item of the questionnaire shown in Figure 6 as emotional appraisal confirm the findings of the preceding five items in the questionnaire. The percentages of preference for the first and the second choice here, 3.3% and 6.6% respectively, were astonishingly low compared to the negatively affected third and fourth choices, 33.3% and 20% respectively. It clearly shows that the number of student respondents who idealized (3.3%) or sympathized (6.6%), if they are taken together, with the character of Ram as the hero of the Ramayana was far less than the number of students who responded otherwise (89.9%). The percentage of students who said they did not idealize (33.3%) or sympathize (20%) with Ram as the hero of the Ramayana, if they are taken together (53.3%), was even greater than the percentage of students who preferred not to be very articulate about their options and preferred to state otherwise (36.6%). These figures showed a very conclusive picture of the disinclination among the student respondents of the present study to idealize or to sympathize with the character of Ram. This disinclination to idealize and to sympathize with the character of Ram as the hero of the Ramayana in a way explained the lack of special motivation for the preference of the name 'Ram' in the context of the other associative environments that had been presented in the preceding items of the questionnaire.

What do all these figures implicate about the familiarity and the popularity of the name 'Ram' among the contemporary youths of the state? It may fairly safely be concluded that the youths of the states are familiar with the name 'Ram' and they also associate the name 'Ram' with positive values. It may appear encouraging to people who dream about inculcating a positive awareness about Ram among the contemporary youths of the state. But the strictly religious implications of Ram may not be shared by the educated young generation of the state. The reluctance to prefer the example sentences with the name 'Ram' at the subject position, when the associative environments were related to cultural fields familiar to them, shows a lack of special emotional pull often seen with objects, individuals or events that capture their imagination. The non-preference for the name 'Ram' when the names of the example sentences were associated with the attributes of goodness and honesty also point to a similar attitude. In fact, the shilly-shallying attitude shown by the educated youths of the state to emulate and idealize 'Ram' by sympathizing with the character of Ram in the Ramayana may confirm the fact that the name 'Ram' may be familiar to them, since it is an important cultural presence in the state, but the name is not or has not been popular enough to cancel out the vacillation. The name 'Ram' may well be associated with positive values, but it may only be perceived so more in terms of associations with myths and legends than with anything else.

References

1. Herman, David. "Narrative: Cognitive Approaches." Encyclopedia of Language and Linguistics, 2nd dition, edited by Keith Brown, et al., section edited by Cathrine Emmott, 452-59. Oxford:Elsevier, 2006.
2. Herman, David, ed. Narrative Theory and the Cognitive Sciences. Stanford, CA: CSLI Publications, 2003.
3. Hogan, Patrick Colm. The Mind and Its Stories: Narrative Universals and Human Emotion. Cambridge: Cambridge Univ. Press, 2003.
3. Lee, Penny. "'Feelings of the mind' in Talk about Thinking in English." Cognitive Linguistics 14 (2003):221-49.
4. Levin, Janet. "Qualia." In The MIT Encyclopedia of the Cognitive Sciences, edited by Robert A. Wilson and Frank C. Keil, 693–94. Cambridge, MA: MIT Press, 1999.
5. Talmy, Leonard. Toward a Cognitive Semantics, vols. 1 and 2. Cambridge, MA: MIT Press, 2000.
6. Tannen, Deborah, ed. Framing in Discourse. Oxford: Oxford Univ. Press, 1993. 221–49.

प्रदेश
2019
प्रयागराज

Chapter V

Reading Sita's tale from North-east India : Counter Traditions and Textual Blasphemies

Saurva Sengupta

Ramayana continues to influence the socio-cultural dimensions of the North-east, like it does in other parts of India. But, in North-east India, the main story lines are permeated by verbal prose narratives, oral songs, mantras (charms) etc drawn from local traditions and cultural milieus. Also, the predominant literary texts are seen as elitist, patriarchal and regressive and are altered by populist, subaltern and feminist versions. Our paper argues that Ramayana in North-east India is modulated around the figure of Sita, as Shakti-the active female principle and so offers a counter reading to the north-Indian texts, with their principle action woven around the figure of the male protagonist. For example, the Tiwas, are an ethnic tribe that inhabit parts of Nagaon and even the hill tracts of Meghalaya. In their version of Ramayana, Tiwa Rama was the king of Ayodhya and Sita was his wife. The legend says that during her tenure of banishment Sita gave birth to two sons-Lava and Kush. When Rama came to know about this, he with his brother in disguise visited the hermitage where Sita and the boys were staying. As Rama was eagerly looking at his children, Sita entered the scene, sweeping the courtyard and out of rage and vanity, she threw off the rubbish at them. Such treatment of the males by females is common in this society. A Tiwa woman generally supports this kind of behavior with the statement: "that's O.K. It happens. Such type of man deserves such type of treatment" (Maheswar Neog 330). Another belief among the Tiwas is that there should be an earthquake at the end of Ramayana just to indicate the exit of Sita into mother earth. So, the Tiwa Ramayana singer abstains from telling the whole of Ramayana because he is afraid that the whole world may be destroyed. Within this tradition, Rama, is not a God but a god-man who suspects his wife and is reduced to a nobody. As Rama Joshi and Joanna Liddle remarks :

> **Sita's repudiation of Rama comes to represent to the vast majority of the audience, not merely a wife refusing a husband, but an expression of a socially acceptable and highly sublimated act of counter-aggression against a figure of authority... [In contrast with Draupadi's aggression that] is directed outwards — towards her husbands, especially Yudhishthira..., Sita... expresses her anger at her love object inwardly, and this manner of aggression, i.e., through masochistic actions, appears to be more socially normative in ancient and modern India for both men and women (36).**

In another part of the story, found in Nagaon and Darrang, after returning from Lanka, Sita was sleeping in a cot. She was pregnant then. Rama had a sister who caused Sita to wake up and give a description of the demon king Ravana, which she was reluctant to do. However, she decided to draw a picture of Ravana, using areca nut on the floor. However, as ill luck would have it, in the mean time, Ram came in. He saw the picture made by Sita. It led him to conclude that Sita could not forget Ravana till date. Hence Rama decided finally to banish her (Jaydipsinh Dodiya Critical Perspectives 147).

With these diversity of approaches, the story of Rama subvert, reject and even overthrow "certain relations of power and religious claims" (Questioning Ramayanas 2). They for example ask: why only the Brahmin males allowed to interpret and read the sacred scriptures and the women just reduced to the position of devotees? Or as the Jains ask "how can monkeys vanquish the powerful raksasa warriors like Ravana[...]. They are lies and contrary to reason." (A.K. Ramanujan 10). The Jaina Ramayana composed by Vimalasuri believes that Ravana is a great man undone by his admiration and love for Sita, which finally lets him down and which he cannot resist. Such variations have political implications because as Richman argues there are three different reasons-a) it establishes the ideal of Ramraj, a polity "whose king practices absolute justice, maintains order, preserves stability and ensures the prosperity of the kingdom, as these functions are set out in the dharmashastras b) because the devotees praises Rama as maryadapurushottama (the ideal man), Rama's story present a set of values from which definitions of caste, gender relations and even social organizations will follow. Finally, because the visions present in them are utopian, they are likely to take the people and the power elites to deny parity to 'others'. Even within the ambit of Valmiki's Ramayan, some of Rama's actions prove illogical or ill-considered. These include his killing of Vali from behind for which the latter castigates Rama for violating the warrior code; his mutilation of Surpankha, even though she is a female; his killing of Shambuka because he performed ascetic practices reserved for a social superior; his desire to examine the purity of Sita and his decision to banish her even after knowing about her pregnancy. While such ambiguities, cannot be easily glossed over, the rationale of interpretations is admissible when texts are indicative, says Richman of hegemony or allows for subversion of status quo.

Such oppositional text prove similarly that the Aryans were just one of the many races who came to inhabit India. These include the Mongoloids, the Indo-Aryans, the Australoids or Austric and the Dravidians, the last being a very minor group representing a migrant population. They do not read the original Sanskrit and are also not interested in brahminism. They examine the text as codifying ideal some set of relations. Thus, the north-east tribals and their versions of Rama's story expresses the 'other' perspective-the subaltern here constituted of the 'adivasis' or the 'vanabasis' who unlike much of India have not relegated woman to subservient positions. K.R.Srinivasa Iyengar observes that folk versions of the story emphasize upon Sita's suffering because it seeks to "bring out the dignity of the Indian woman in its full splendor" and also to "make out a lonely man of Rama, so that he may become more human, more intimate and more a person belonging to ourselves (107). This assessment of Prof Iyengar while being admirable is still limited to advocating a traditional view. This is proved when Sita confronts Ravana in his palace pleasure garden and defends herself by upholding the patriarchical notion that her sexuality belongs to her husband alone. However, as Sutherland Goldman points out, as soon as Ravana leaves, Sita despairs because Rama has not yet saved her. She is also terrorized to realize the dependence of woman upon man's power (qtd. Richman 108). From this perspective, the northeast versions of the Rama story may be less Hindu than the Hindu versions of north India. But, this difference may also have to do with the tribal belief in the great-mother, the equivalent of Kali in tantra.

The Karbis have their own version of the Ramayana. According to a scholar, a Kachari King Mahamanikya ruled the area comprising of the Kolong-Kapili valley when Madhava Kandali completed the translation of the Ramayana under the patronage of this king. So, the Ramakatha contained in the Sabin Alun is the echo of the Ramayana translated by Madhava Kandali. This version of the story says that Rama was sent to exile in the Narajon (Narayan) Hills where the bird Womu (Jatayu), was also cremated. The Rama of Sabin Alun tried to end his life by jumping in the funeral pyre. At this juncture, Lakshmana brought water from the river Deopani in a polo, a fishing implement, and doused the fire of the funeral pyre. Later on both the brothers took bath in the Deopani and set out to rescue Sita. It is interesting that Janaka here is just another farmer, who sits on top of a "tongi" a makeshift hut built on top of a tree and monitors his cultivation. His wife Hemphi keeps her important belongings in a khaloi, a container made of bamboo and is meant to keep fishes when fishing. Here, Janaka, keeps the egg of a peahen from which Sita is born. Sita is however just a simple girl, who carries food to her father in the fields and looks after her household property.

Nabaneeta Dev Sen, noted scholar and critic says that most tribal versions of the Ramayana developed after the sanskritization of local people. Yet most tribals, identify with the disempowered and claim to have descended either from Ravana, Sita and Kumbhakarna. The Karbi Ramayana Sabin Alun is the Song of Sita. Sen adds that the tribals:

> **[...] look upon Sita as the essential orphan and see Rama as the oppressor. Whether he is a king or a god, Rama remains distant, inaccessible and unaccountable for his acts. Rama is the representative of the brahminical-feudal system, whereas Sita is a child of nature, just like the tribals themselves (Alternative Interpretations of Ramayana)**

The Karbi Ramayan alludes to one incident where Rama has to perform a certain puja. Only two people could perform this puja- Bali and Ravana. As Bali was dead, Rama had to prostrate before Ravana, who performed the ritual process. Laxmana was extremely annoyed at this. Rama explained, that it was not to Ravana but to the priest that he was paying his respects. Ravana blesses Rama in pure priestly tradition. Sen in her explanation says that here, the brahminical value system is itself employed "to subvert the classical relationship between Rama and Ravana in order to make Rama bow down to the generosity of Ravana" (Sen Alternative Interpretations). Sen also quotes another version of the text, where after her marriage, Sita stays back at King Janaka's household and Rama stays with his young wife as a gharjamai. Laxman gives company to Ram and both assist Janaka in his jhum cultivation, a typical practice among the tribals. Sen finally mentions a Mech version of Ramayana, discovered in the north-east in `1958. This version explains the conflict between the Hindus and Muslims to the fight between the sons of Rama and Laxman. The Mech tribals believe that Laxman, after eating beef became a Muslim. His children Hasaan and Hussein were killed by Lava and Kush, because of their divergent faiths and ideological conditioning.

Adbhut Ramayana, composed by Raghunatha Mahanta, tells the story of Sita, after she has entered the earth. It describes how in the underworld, she misses her two sons Lava and Kusha and requests the great snake Basukhi, who is also her mother to bring them to her. The next sections describes Hanuman's fight with the snake and his success in getting them back to Ayuodha. This story, says Mahanta was derived from the Adbhuta Kanda, composed by rishi Markendya. Dr. Nabinchandra Sarma in his book "Puroni Asomiyar Sahitoyor Sourabh" (171) discredits Mahanta completely and argues that Mahanata may have derived his story from Ramsaraswati, who confessed to have sourced his Badhkavyaas from various Sanskrit sources like Shiv Rahasya etc. when such sources have not been discovered. While this argument makes Mahanta an accomplice with Ramsaraswati in forging un-Ramayana stories, Sarma confesses that Valmiki is conspicuously silent in describing Sita after she enters the underworld. He stops short of saying that Valmiki like Tulsidas was too devoted to Rama to go beyond his grand narrative plan and admits that writers have to invent or trace myths to some ancestors in order to convince ordinary readers. Matters stand on their head when Valmiki's Ramayana is credited as an work that collects relevant data from public memory while Mahanta is relegated as a mere "surprise" who caters to unlettered readers. It may be remarked that when Sankardeva and Madhavdeva rewrote the Ramayana, they did not rely upon the Sanskrit original entirely. W.L. Smith has this to say:

> **Madhavdea's Adikanda is rich in non-Valmikian stories and in the Uttrakanda, Sankardeva concentrates on the story of Rama's reputation of Sita and omits much else. His story is remarkable for its strong sympathy with Sita (Ramayana Revisited 90).**

However, when Ananta Kandali revised Madhav Kandals version of the epic, he made sure that he did not mention any other deities except Vishnu. Whether this had to do with a need to streamroll ethnic or gender differences between the northeast and the rest of India or to tiptoe a grand pan Asian narrative out of political compulsion cannot be discerned. The Sanskrit Adbhut Ramayan, illustrates the superiority of goddess to Rama. Infact, the Brhaddharma and Mahabhagavata Puranas tell a story of how Hanuman convinces the goddess to withdraw her protection from Lanka on condition that Rama offers her autumnal worship. This Ramayana makes the same point in a much more dramatic fashion. It tells how Sita provokes Rama to fight the much mightier thousand-headed Ravana, who rules the island of Pusfikara. Rama takes up the challenge only to be slained by the demon, whereupon Sita transforms herself into Kali and destroys Ravana and his army" (W.L.Smith 96). In Assam, there is a similar version of the story and it is found in the anonymous play called the "Sataskandha Ravana Vadha" (the demon has only one hundred heads here). In Raghunath Mahanta's version too, there is mention of Sita both as benign nurturer and as horrific destroyer, both as Sita and Kali.

Maruti bodti Suna Bhogowati
Sureswari Broteswari
Sristir Karini Jogot Tarini
Asa lila tonudhari
Abidyaswarup Jeev Samostok
Sonsar Nikare niya
Bidyarupe ponu Tumi Bhogowati
Sonshar Tariya niya
Jehi rupe bhabe Sehi rupe pabe
Tumi Jogotor Mata
Tumi Sorbo srestha Tumi sorbo presta
Tumi Sorbolok data

(Qtd. Nabinchandra Sarma Puroni Asomiya Sahitya, 177).

Elsewhere, in the same work, Hanuman says:

Jodi Ram kaal Tumi Kali jano saar
Amat Kohibe matri nolagoy aar

(*Qtd. Nabinchandra Sarma 177*).

The lines quoted above recalls the Sanskrit version were chastised by sages for having involved Rama in a debacle, Sita picks up her unconscious husband's bow and arrows. She takes the form of Kali and destroys her opponent.

Bellowing at the mighty, valorous demon,
Laughing boisterously and loudly, Sita, daughter of Janak
The goddess, who has many hideous forms, abandoned her own form (svarup)
(And took on a form) fit for killing...
Gaunt, with sunken eyes that whirled in circles,
With anklets made of bone, fearsome, invincible in valour and speed,
Harsh-voiced,... with lolling tongue...,
She was as black as the ocean at the time of Pralay.
Carrying bell and noose, sword and shield,
She jumped down quickly from her chariot
And fell on Ravan's chariot like a hawk.
In a flash she playfully lopped off Ravan's
Thousand heads with her sword.

(Carman, John Braisted. The Theology of Ramanuja 13)

Unfortunately, the Bhakti tradition never accepted the Tantric view that the Consort of Narayana was the active creative principle in Her own right, the

Shakti. For example Sarma suggests that Raghunatha Mahanta here equates Sita with Shakti only to bridge the divide between Vaishnav and tantra movements. So, even when Sita is seen in terms of Shakti, "there is rarely any suggestion that she is dominant over Rama, or even equal to Him" (Frank Whaling 198-99). The cults of Shiva and Krishna are however free from such overriding male hierarchies and allow the free play of "eroticism and asceticism." In the character of Rama, "sexuality is almost completely suppressed" (Paula Richman 82). So, while Rama suffers his detachment from Sita, he expresses to Hanuman his paternal need to get back his sons:

> **Sriram bolosto baap suniyo maruti**
> **Sitar biyoge huwa asuho bishruti**
> **Putror biyoge pran dhorite napari**
> **Rokha kora putra sok agoni udhari**

Through such examples, Sita and Hanuman become tour de forces- active agencies of control and direction. Rama is passive. Sita is Prakriti and expresses the Shakti tendencies. Hanuman is the skillful warrior. His movements through the various layers of the netherworld is an important component in this story. Rama, when describing Hanuman refers to the latter's "yog sadhya maya" the force of illusion pertaining to yoga or meditative practices: "ontobine hitosthan/jaibak napare aan" (Sharma 173). But, Hanuman can only appease Sita-the great mother goddess by reciting various "stutis" followed by hymns in her honor. Hanuman's journey to the underworld, the image of Basuki and snakes etc can only be understood as indicative of the Kundalini, the symbolic mother energy suggested in tantra. In this organically interrelated vision — this "universe of bhakti" — "the tasks of this world are no longer opposed to the work of deliverance, they lead to it." In tantric sacrifice, the victim is seen as substitute for the sacrificier, i.e. should cost something to the sacrificier. Tantra allowed for a relationship between power and purity- between the pure Brahmin, and the powerful king, where the sacrificial ritual, served as a key exchange of material and symbolic capital between the pure priest and the powerful king (Romila Thapar 312).

Rama makes it when he offers his eye to please the goddess but cannot endure his twins taken away. When he prays to Shakti, in his fight with Ravana, he seeks her for a time-bound political gain and importantly to defeat an enemy Ravan, who always sought her but did not get her in a failed Oedipus fling. In the second instance, he asks Hanuman to appease the Goddess for him, thereby suggesting either his personal inadequacy or a dilution of his trust on her. Hanuman follows Rama when he feigns "death" in his fight with the snakes. Feigning is a difficult word here expressing a loss or giving up. So, when it is heard that Hanuman has been killed at the hands of Bojronemi, brother of Kalinemi, Sita expresses her surprise:

Janaki boloi Heneki howai
Soshar mathat sring
Koit dekhi suni Asa Apuni
Kukure Maroi Shingho

So, if Sita gives in to the wish of Hanuma, it had also to do with her love and devotion for her husband. Hanuman's penance and devotion for Rama was again good enough to substitute for any penance or dissimulation:

Pobon Tonoi Sorbote Ḍurjoy
Ramor Sebok bora
Lavat Kushot Kori Abirot
Tat mor doa chora

So, Valmiki's demure princess and heroine is central to all the actions in the epic. She causes this when she asks Rama to go after the golden deer and is kidnapped by Ravana. Then she waits upon her husband to fulfill his mission of rescuing her when she could have done so herself. This reveals a lady who is more complex and evolving than her husband. Valmiki praises her both as knowledge and ignorance-the kundalini-which is subterraneous and disruptive of accepted reason. Unfortunately, Valmiki stops short of giving her extended attention and just multiples her names. So, Ramayana remains the story of Rama. Sita, is a very important part of this story. But, she is just one of the characters.

Raghunatha Mahanta's book ends abruptly with Sita castigated by her sons and Basuki similarly blamed and thoroughly ostracized by Hanuman. Scholars and critics see this end as ill-conceived and even pandering to common tastes. But, an assumption would be that a order suggested around the mother is disruptive of traditional hierarchies-brahminism, caste and dynasty identities to begin with. But, at a different level of analysis, a child moves gradually away from its mother and steps into the world of father either out of compulsion or because it make economic or at least a political sense to do so. Yet, it never fully disassociates itself from the mother. Zizek call this experience a kind of oscillation "the excluded intersection of the two sets" (The Puppet and the Dwarf 69¬), when the child knows that it neither belongs to itself-the subject or to the object-the mother. Lacan describes it through his notion of "extimacy" (external plus intimate) when the possibility of absence, gives presence its security i.e when the present is bearable only when the mother is not around or is absent.

However, in Indian philosophy, the great mother is also the non-ego, the feminine unconscious, who cannot be possessed but who must unite with Siva for a blissful union. So, if Hanuman is the cause that unites Rama and Sita, he could be seen as link that makes such union possible. Yet, his abrupt change of behavior that borders on madness or hysteria could have a possible explanation: madness that results from psychic disorientation after the rise of the serpent or Kundalini within. What is also significant is that this consciousness of the great mother should come intrinsically, without which it runs the risk of a psycho-technical externalization. When such a prayer is continuous, counting is of no importance. Unfortunately, as Raghunath Mahanta describes Hanuman's journey to the underworld, the only signs of progress are the names of planes or zones, a veritable system: "patal, rasatol, talatal, bitol, atol etc." Considering that Hanuman is also a great illusionist, his hymns to Sita and then his ill behavior to Basuki etc would correspond ambiguously between two different planes of consciousness- the rational ego, which seeks to possess the mother and even control her as a material object and the non-ego, where the mother is symbolized as nature, requiring a constant internalization of her love and affections. But, Hanuman fails in this. Instead, one can fall back upon Laxman, who sees Rama's failure as a king in his inability to treat Sita with reverence:

Amakhar baikyo nushunila kishuman
Abe khed kora tumi kikhor nidan
Janokik dila tumi joto apoman
Tak sohibak pare kahar poran
Budhimonto pundit kichu noi
Ki Koribe Iswar sehise sotiyo hoi
Heno jani dada tejiyok sobe roch
Ashar sonsar jani huwok sontosh

(*Sarma Purani Axamiya Sahityara Saurabha 175*)

So, the denunciation of the feminine or mother is a cause of political and social paralysis. Rama's devotion to the gods or even his deep knowledge of the scriptures are quantitative external solutions. Laxman's analysis of Rama's failure bear also on the conduct of Hanuman whose knowledge of scriptures and admiration for his hero are equally flawed or doomed.

René Girard in his Violence and the Sacred (1977) says that ritual sublimates violence on the stage and thereby ensures that social hierarchies are maintained (qtd. Schechener The Future of Ritual 234). When this fails, violence takes over. Schechner also alludes to Freud, who in analyzing children observed that young people hallucinate when they believe that their thoughts can achieve everything. Their minds are more sensitive to the unconscious. Within such parameters, Lava and Kusha's violent treatment of Sita at the end of Adbhuta Ramayana may be described as "mimicry" "irony" and "repetition" (Bhabha, Mimicry and Men: The Ambivalence of Colonial Discourse 23). Mimicry also indicates a "mockery" and an ironic compromise according to Bhaba between the panoptical desire for dominance and the counter pressure of change. While Sita was made a scapegoat for immediate political gains earlier, her ill treatment by her sons and by Hanuman towards Basuki mocks her power to be a model and implies a continuation of that narrative logic, wherein a society creates sacrificial victims. Unfortunately, as Girard argues, violence and sexuality are connected: "the shift from violence to sexuality and from sexuality to violence is easily effected, even by the most normal of individuals, totally lacking in perversion. Thwarted sexuality leads naturally to violence, just as lovers' quarrels often end in an amorous embrace" (Girard 37).

Conclusion

The north-east presents different versions of the Ramayana story, much of which run against and opposite to canonical sanskrit verses. The interest lies both in the stories themselves as also in a desire for a holistic interpretation of the epic. The argument for Sita would also reflect a modern concern with aggression and its counter that is sublimated through a concern for the feminine as agents of change. If the traditional text vouchsafes for Sita as a woman of dignity who suffers in silence, a mere victim of power and political necessity, who does not turn into a predator, the versions in the north-east does the opposite. Here, she is a warrior who fights without inhibitions.

Primary Sources

1. Dr. Sarma, Nabin Chandra. Purani Axamiya Sahityara Saurabha. Guwahati:
   Chandra Prakash, 1996.

Secondary Sources

2. Appadurai, Korom, and Wendy Doniger (ed.), Purana Perennis: Reciprocity and Transformation in Hindu and Jain Texts. Albany: State University of New York Press, 1993.
3. Biardeau, Madeleine and Charles Malamoud. Hinduism: The Anthropology of a Civilization. Paris: Flammarion, 1981.
4. Brown, C. Mackenzie. The Triumph of the Goddess:The Canonical Models and Theological Visions of the Devi Bhagavata Purana. Albany: State University of New York Press, 1990.

5. Carman, John Braisted. The Theology of Ramanuja (New Haven and London: Yale University Press, 1974. Print.
6. Datta, Birendranath. Cultural Contours of North East India. New Delhi: OUP, 2012. Print.
7. Devsharma, Sree Dharanikanta. The Holy Shrine of Kamakhya. Guwahati: The Author, 1999.
8. Eliade, Mircea. Yoga: Immortality and Freedom. Princeton: Princeton University Press, 1971.
9. Goswami, Basanta Kumar Deva. A Critical Study of the Ramayana. Guwahati: Punthi Pustak, 1994.
10. Iyengar, K.R Srinivasa. Asian Variations in Ramayana: Their Cultural, Social and Anthropological Significance: Conference Proceedings. New Delhi: Sahitya Academy, 1981. Print.
11. Joydipsinh, Dodiya., ed. Critical Perspectives on the Ramayana. New Delhi: Swarup & Son, 2001. Print.
12. Madhu Kishwar and Ruth Vanita, In Search of Answers: Indian Women's Voices from Manushi. London: Zed Books, 1984. Print.
13. Preston, J. Mother Worship: Theme and Variations. (Chapel Hill: The University of North Carolina Press, 1982. Print.
14. Sarma, Satyendranath. A History of Assamese Literature. Otto Harrasowitz: Wiesbaden, 1976.
15. Sen, Nabaneeta. Alternative Versions of Ramayana. Calcutta:
16. Stuart H. Blackburn and A.K. Ramanujan., ed. Another Harmony: New Essays on the Folklore of India. Berkeley: University of California Press, 1986.
17. Wendy Doniger O'Flaherty, Asceticism and Eroticism in the Mythology of Shiva. London: Oxford University Press, 1973.
18. Richman, Paula. Many Ramayanas: the Diversity of a Narrative Tradition in South Asia. Los Angles: California UP, 1991. Print.
19. Ramanujan,,A.K, Vinay Dharwadker,, Stuart H. Blackburn. The Collected Essays of A.K. Ramanujan. London and New Delhi: OUP, 2004. Print.
20. Schechner, Richard. The Future of Ritual: Writings on Culture and Performance. London & NY: Rutledge, 1993. Print.
21. Thapar,Romila. Imagined Religious Communities: Ancient History and the Modern Search for a Hindu Identity. New Delhi: Critical Quest, 2004. Print.
22. Whaling, Frank. The Rise of Religious Significance of Rama. New Delhi: Motilal Banarsidass, 1980. Print.

Chapter VI

Ram in the Writings of Sankardeva : A Comparative Study

(With special reference to Kirtan-Ghosa, Bargeet and Ram-Bijay)

Dr. Hari Prasad Baruah

Sankardeva (1449-1568 A.D.) was a versatile genius in the annals of Indian History. He was a poet, social- religious reformer, playwright, actor, musician and an ardent devotee. He is regarded as the fore-runner of the Bhakti Movement that took its rise in India. Sankardeva visited almost all the temples and holy shrines of both northern and southern India. He came into contact with Vaishnavite teachers of various schools at these sacred places. He had many theological and learned discussions with them. After gathering knowledge, he introduced "Ekasharannaamdharma" in Assam. He studied the literary pieces that were in Sanskrit and on that basis he composed a number of literary pieces. His compositions may be classified as1 –

1. **Kavya (Poetry) :** *(i) Harischandra Upakhyan, (ii) Rukmini - Haran Kavya, (iii) Bali Chalan, (iv) Amrit Manthan, (v) Ajamil Upakhyan and (vi) Kurukshetra.*
2. **Books reflecting " Bhakti-tatva" :** *(i) Bhakti Pradip, (ii) Bhakti Ratnakar (Sanskrit) and (iii) Nimi-Navasiddha Sangbad*
3. **Translative:** *(i) Bhagavat 1st, 2nd, 6th (Ajamil Upakhyan Matra) 8th (Balichalan, Amrit Mathan) 10th, 11th, 12th Skandha and (ii) Uttarakand Ramayana.*
4. **Ankiya Naat :** *(i) Patni Prasad, (ii) Kaliya Daman, (iii) Keli Gopal, (iv) Rukmini-Haran, (v) Parijat-Haran and (vi) Rama Bijaya.*
5. **Devotional Songs:** *(i) Bargeet and (ii) Bhatima, (iii) Totaya and Chapaya.*
6. **Naam-Prasang :** *(i) Kirtan Ghosa and (ii) Gunamala*

This paper endeavours to focus Ram in Sankardeva's writings with special reference to *Kirtan-Ghosa, Bargeet* and *Ram-Bijay.*

The study is limited to Sankardeva's Kirtan-Ghosa, Bargeet and Ram-Bijaya. Three printed books are considered as texts.They are 1. Kirtan-Ghosa

(Published by Srimanta Sankardeva Sangha), 2. Bargeet (Edited by Bap Chandra Mahanta) and 3. Rama Bijaya Naat (Edited by Keshabananda Deva Goswami).

Kirtan-Ghosa

Kirtan-Ghosa is the outstanding literary production of Sankardeva. The Kirtan-Ghosa printed in the present day comprises of 27 full-fledged khanda or chapters. Each of the chapters depicts different story or a subject-matter. The chapter contains 1 to 22 kirtanas. One noteworthy point is that Sankardeva wrote the Kirtan-Ghosa in different periods of time. Each of the chapters could not be compiled into a single book during Sankardeva's lifetime. Later on, after Sankardeva's demise, his disciple Madhabdeva had them arranged and compiled by his nephew Ramcharan Thakur. The present study includes the following chapters of Kirtan-Ghosa : 1) Chaturbingxoti-Avatar-Varnana, 2) Naam-aparadh, 3) Paxanda-Mardan, 4) Dhyaan-Varnan, 5) Ajamilopakhyan, 6) Prahlad Charitra, 7) Gajendra Upakhyan, 8) Hara-Mohan, 9) Bali-Chalan, 10) Sishu-Lila, 11) Raas-Krida, 12) Kansa-Badh, 13) Gopi-Uddhav Sangbad, 14) Kujir Bancha Puron, 15) Akrurar Bancha Puron, 16) Jarasandhar Juddho, 17) Kaaljavan-Badh, 18) Musukunda-Stuti, 19) Shyamantaka Haran, 20) Naradar Krishna-Darshan, 21) Bipra Putra Ananay, 22) Damodar- Biprakhyan, 23) Daivakir Putra-Anayan, 24) Vedastuti, 25) Lilamala, 26) Sri Krishnar Baikuntha-Prayaan and 27) Bhagavat- Tatparjya.

The religion of Sankardeva is known as Eksharan Naamdharma. The main principle of this religion is Ek Sharan (supreme surrender to the one). This theology has been derived from Gita's 'Sarvadharmanaparitajya Mamekang Sharanang Braja'2. Sankardeva followed the Bhakti Marg in order to preach this theology. As regards Bhakti, it is classified into nine types. Among the nine types of Bhakti, Sankardeva mainly followed Sravan- Kirtan. Sankardeva truly believed Adaita Brahma of Vedanta.3 That means his goal is Brahma of Vedanta. He starts the Kirtan-Ghosa by praying to that Brahma – "Prathame Pranamo Brahmarupi Xanatana". Krishna is the base to feel that Brahma. The Krishna here is the Krishna of Bhagabata who is purest Chaitanyamaya Bhagavan or Vishnu. The meaning of Vishnu is omnipresent. The omnipresent Vishnu is Krishna of Gokul, Vrindavan and Mathura. Krishna is regarded as the Purnavatar or the complete incarnation of Vishnu. Sankardeva insisted on the worship of this Purnavatar Krishna. The derivative meaning of Krishna is – cause of joy in this earth. Krishna is Sat Chit Anandamay. The main motto of Sankardeva's Bhakti Dharma is to surrender to Krishna and to do Kirtan-Sravana on his name.

One noteworthy point regarding Kirtan-Ghosa is that Ram has been mentioned everywhere equally with Krishna. Different names have been mentioned in Kirtan-Ghosa to symbolize God such as Hari, Vishnu, Govinda, Narayana, Keshaba, Ram and so on. In spite of these names Krishna, Hari and Ram are the superior names. Naam Prasang, singing of devotional songs, singing of Ghosa and reading Kirtana – all these performances begin with the raga "Krishna Hari Ram". Naam-Kirtana ends with the recital of the name of Ram, Hari and Krishna as well. During prayer, the devotees proceed with Hari Dhvani (utterance of the name of Hari) chanting the names of Hari and Ram. The three names 'Krishna, Hari Ram' is sometimes meditated as Chari Naam (four names). At that moment, these names are meditated as "Krishna Krishna Hari Ram".4

The significance of the name of 'Ram' as described by Madhabdeva in his 'Naam Ghosa' is as follows:

Sadananda Atma Chaitanya Anante
Jihetu Jugi Ramaya /
Etekese Ram Pade Parabrahma
Rupaka Buli Nischaya //179//
Chaitanya Swarupe Jihetu Sadaye
Ramawanta Jagataka /
Etekese Ram Sumadhura Pade
Buli Jana Iswaraka //180//

According to this Ghosa – thy name is Ram where the Sadhaka or Yogis concentrate or do ramana. The Ram Pada signifies Parambrahma. The Chaitanya Swaroop Ram showers happiness and joy on the whole Universe. Therefore, the word 'Ram' is regarded as the name of God. Each Pada of the Kirtana echoes the name of this 'Ram'.

The Kirtan-Ghosa comprises of 27 chapters with 168 Ghosas or refrains. There 'Ram' has been mentioned in 93 Ghosas (as 'Ram' 142 times, as 'SiriRam'/ 'Sri Ram' 4 times and as 'Raghupati' 4 times.)

Ram has been mentioned in the first Ghosa of the first Kirtan of the first chapter of the Kirtan-Ghosa as:

Ghosa// Jaya Hari Gobinda Narayan Ram Keshaba Hari
Ram Ram Keshaba Hari //1//

Ram has been described as the incarnation of Narayana in the 2nd Kirtan of 'Chaturbingsati Avatara' as:

Siri Ram Rupe Kausalyata Avatari
Banabasa Khapila Pitrir Bakya Dhori
Biradha Kavandha Marichara Loila Pran
Khara Dusanaka Prabhu Korila Nirjyana
Ekapata Xore Baali Xaskalila Jiva

Tumharo Prasade Raja Bhailanta Sugriva
Lankata Poxila Sagarata Bandhi Xetu
Bodhila Ravana Sita Haranara Hetu
Bodhila Ranata Aanu Rakshasa Aneka
Bhakta Bibhisanaka Korila Abhisheka
Agnita Porikhya Aani Korila Sitaka
Brahma Deve Stuti Baani Bulila Tumhaka
Xomborila Sita Dasharathara Basane
Ayudhyaka Aaxila Xobharjye Rangamane
Korilaha Rajya Dasha Hajara Batsar
Loge Swarge Nila Xowe Ayodhya Nagar //11//

In the above mentioned Kirtana, the story of Ramayana or the character of Ram has not been described in detail. 'Sri Ram avatara' or the person Ram has been mentioned in the context of describing Narayana's avatara. The Ram avatara is also referred in another part of Kirtan-Ghosa:

Janakir Hetu Bandhilaha Xetu
Dohila Lanka Nagari
Ravanar Maath Katilaha Nath
Aanila Sita Uddhari
Aage Nisinilu Ebese Janilu
Tente Tumi Siri Ram
Agyanika Muk a Prabhu Khyomiyuka
Charane Koru Pranam //1439//

Most importantly, in both of the above mentioned Kirtanas, the incarnated person has been mentioned as 'Siri Ram', not as 'Ram'. Apart from this, Ram mentioned in other parts of Kirtana glorifies the name of God. Since Kirtan-Ghosa was composed to preach the religion of Naam Dharma, therefore, Ram has been used as the synonym of Krishna.

Sankardeva's religion is based on the Juga Dharma. In the 'Paxanda Mardan' the third chapter of Kirtan-Ghosa Sankardeva said that salvation can be gained only through Dhyaan Samadhi in Satya Yuga, Yajna in Treta Yuga, Puja in Dwapar and Kirtan in Kali Yuga. This Kirtan is in the name of Ram:

Satya Juge Kori Dhyan Samadhi/
Tretato Xamasta Jagye Aradhi//
Dwapore Puji Nana Bhakti Bhave/
Kolita Kirtane Xi Gati Pawe //74//
... ...
Kolira Loka Aati Papamati/

Noxadhoi Aan Dharmme Aaro Gati//
Ram Naam Jitu Xotote Gawe/
Xehixe Hatote Mukuti Pawe //78//

The nature of Param Tatva or the Supreme God worshipped in the Kirtana has been described by transcending the primary meaning of words. The symbol of the nature of Param Tatva is Ram. This name i.e. Ram is much more powerful than the Avatari Purush Ram. There is limitation of power in Shagunalila.5 But the pure Supreme Being who is unbound by the limit of natural quality is known as Ram. This is a symbolic name. There is absence of limitation of power of this name. In Madhabdeva's Nam-ghosa, he has mentioned that Ram Naam is more powerful than Ram himself - "He Prana Prabhu Raghupati Ram Ram Ram Ram Ram Tumhaata Koriya Taju Guna Naam Saara" (Pada 640)

Ram Naam is associated with the style of singing of Kirtan. Pada Kirtan begins with Ram Naam and ends with the hymn of Hari and Ram.

The fourth Kirtan of Paxanda Mardan starts with the Ghosa mentioned below:

Ghosa // Ramexe Jibana Ramexe Praana/
Rama Bina Nahi Bandhava Aana //10//

Though it appears here to be the human incarnation of Ram but in reality it refers to Paramtatva Ram. By going through the next Kirtana one would get the actual meaning. "Tantra Mantra Aanu Drabya Aneka/ Desha Kala Patra Chidra Jateka//Purna Nuhi Jata Yajnara Anga/ Harinnaame Kare Xawe Xuxange //" (123) – The Kirtan starting in this way consists of 23 padas. Each pada contains four lines. Interestingly, there is no mention of the word Ram anywhere in this particular Kirtan that comprises of 92 lines, but it is clearly seen that it starts with Ram Naam. Instead of that, the words Hari has been mentioned 13 times, Krishna 7 times and each of the names such as Murari, Gobinda, Madhab and Bamana just once. The entire Kirtan glorifies God's name and the above mentioned names have been used as gunabasak (referring to God's virtue) words of God. Therefore, there is no difference between Ram and these names. While singing the Pada, Ghosa is repeated and in this way Ram Naam is repeated after certain interval. In a sense, though Ram Naam is not mentioned in the Pada, at the same time the recital of Kirtan is being done in the name of Ram.

Bargeet

The devotional songs composed by Srimanta Sankardeva and Madhabdeva are known as Bargeet. Bargeet is based on high moral and spiritual values.

Therefore such songs are known as 'Bargeet'. 6 Banikanta Kakati praises such devotional songs. He said that there is abundance of songs in ancient literature, but Bargeets are unique in their language and significance. These songs indicated the beginning of a new era in the world of literature and religion.7 After listening to Bargeet, common people get mesmerized by the high spiritual ideology that they contain.

It is well-known that Sankardeva composed 240 Bargeets. But only 35 of these are available now. The spiritual theology of Hinduism such as 'Param Purushuttva' of Krishna, his various incarnations, salvation and the result of Kirtana is the main theme of Sankarḍeva's Bargeet. In Dr. Banikanta Kakati's word-

'Borgeetborar besibhagatei ephale Krishnar param purusatta aru anphale dahjanar ejan hoi manabi-lila prakash – ei dufaliya byakttittar bikash dekha jay... Sankardevar rasita jibor geet etiao ase, sai ataiburai prarthanaxusak. Manabjiban druspraipya athas khyanabhangur aru mayamai; hari-bhakati muhasanna jiban samudrat dhrubatara – eye nana bhab aru bhasat Sankardevar geetborar sadharan tatparya.'[8]

Ram has been mentioned in Sankardeva's Bargeet in two ways – 1. as God's name and 2. as incarnation of God. Ram has been mentioned in 13 Bargeets among the 35. Here (among these 13), Ram has been specifically mentioned as God's name in 12 Bargeets and the rest 1 mentions Ram as incarnation of God.

Ram as the name of God:

The words used in Sankardeva's Bargeet to symbolize God's name are as follows: Jadab, Jalanidhijadhab, Narayan, Gopal, Sarangapani, Kamalapati, Madhab, Hari, Narahari, Gobinda, Hrishikesh, Sripati, Murari, Keshab and Ram. As for instance, Ram Pada has been used to symbolize God in the following way:

1. **Bachane buli Ram Dharam Aratha Kam**
   Mukuti Sukhe Sukhe Payo.
   Sabakahu Param Suhriday Harinaam
   Sute Anta Keri Daayo. Geet – 10
2. **Shori Ram Naam Amiya Upajuga**
   Joise Purisha Sukura Kayu Upajuga / Geet – 13
3. **Ram Naam Moh Nikhila Punya Bahu**
   Uhi Nigam Tatva Baani /
   Kaliku Parama Dharama Harinaam Parhi
   Punu Marama Na Jaani // Geet – 15

4. **Paamaru Man Ram Charane Chitta Dehu /**
   Athira Jivana Ram Madhaba Keri Naam
   Maranaka Xambal Lehu //Geet – 17
5. **Ram Mere Hriday Pankaje Roise/**
   Bhai Chitte Nisintaxa Koise //
   Jaga-Taraka Jakeri Naam/
   Dekhu Xu Punu Apuna Thaam//
   Ram Suhrida Xudara Mata/
   Jaana Ramexe Abhaydata//
   Ram Bhakat Param Nidhi/
   Ram Bine Nahi Aara Siddhi//
   Ram Iha Paraluke Gati/
   Tahe Dekhu Nahi Mandamati//
   Krishna-Kinkara Sankara Bhaana/
   Ram Bine Gati Nahi Aana // Geet – 18

These devotional songs glorify the name of Ram. There is no difference between the names Ram, Hari, Krishna etc.

'Ram' as Incarnation of God

The words used by Sankardeva in his Bargeet to signify the Avatar or the incarnation of the Lord are as follows : Narasingha/Narahari, Gopal/Krishna/ Kanu, Baman and Ram/Raghav/Raghupati. The one and only Bargeet in which there is the depiction of Ram Avatar is as follows:

Dhrum - **Suno Suno Re SuraBairi Pramana**
Nixasara Naaxo Nidana
Raamo Naamo Jama Xamaraka Xaaji
Xamadale Kayali Payana

Pada - **Thata Prakata Patu Kauti Kauti Kopi**
Giri Gara Gara Padaghave
Baridhi Tori Tori Kare Gurutara Giri
Dhori Dhori Samaraka Dhave
Haata Ghaata Bohu Baata Biyapi e
Chaugare Berhala Lanka
Guru Ghana Ghana Ghosa Gharixana Garjana
Srabane Janamaya Sanka
Dheera Beera Surasekhara Raghava
Ravana Tuwapori Jampe
Sura Nara Kinnara Phanadhara Thara Thara
Mahidhara Taraxi Prakampe

Andha Mugudha Dashaskandha Papabudha
Janaki Xirata Sorayee
Raghupati Padabara Dhara Rajanichara
Sankara Kahatu Upaya. (Geet 30)

The above mentioned Bargeet is all about Ram's visit to Lanka with the Banar Sena to rescue Sita from Ravana. At the starting of this Bargeet, Ravana has been addressed – "Suno Suno Re Sura Bairi Pramana/ Nixasara Naaxo Nidana/Raamo Naamo Jama Xamaraka Xaaji/Xamadale Kayali Payana." (Hear! O' hear! The cause of destruction of the night roamers, the veritable foes of the gods, Yama in the form of Ram is arrayed for battle and proceeds) The song ends like this- "Andha Mugudha Dashaskandha Papabudha/Janaki Xirata Soraee/Raghupati Padabara Dhara Rajani Chara/Sankara Kahatu Upaya)" (O' malicious, bewildered Ravana, surrender yourself and be at the feet of Ram with Janaki on thy head. Sankardeva advises this as the only way for you). This is the advice of Sankardeva to Ravana. But interestingly, Ravana is not contemporaneous with Sankardeva. Therefore this particular Borgeet may be considered as symbolic. In this context Bapchandra Mahanta puts forward his views :

"Abidyarup andhakarat bisarn kora dah indriar salak manai Ravan. Manar bax hoi bisairupi banat abaddha hoi thaka jibatmai Sita. Ram paramatmar pratik aru banarsena teor sakti namar (bhaktir) pratik. Nam ba bhaktidharmak lagat loi paramatmai maya ba abidyar bandhanar para jibatmak uddhar kare. Tene abasthat atmasamarpan kartoyei manar kartabya hoi pare."[9]

- It is clear from the above mentioned explanation that Sankardeva glorifies Ram naam in this Bargeet as he addresses Ram.

Ram Bijay

Earlier, songs were used for the purpose of preaching religion in India and were accepted but plays and acting were not accepted for the same. It was Sankardeva, who for the first time introduced acting and plays as the medium of preaching religion. He authored six plays. They are Patni-prasada, Kali-damana, Keli-gopala, Rukmini-harana, Parijata-harana and Ram-bijay. Among these, Ram Bijay or Sita Sayambara is regarded as the last play of Sankardeva. This play was composed in 1490 Saka and this has been mentioned in a sloka at the last part of the play. 10 This is considered as the single piece of drama based on Ramayana's story. The other plays of Sankardeva are centered in Krishna. Ram Bijay is the single most play where Ram is the main character.

The story of Ram Bijay is there in Adi Kanda Ramayana. The Pancham Adhyaya (fifth chapter) of Agni Puran has the same story in it. According to Maheshwar Neog, the plot of Ram Bijay play has been extracted from Bal Kanda Ramayana; there is a light shade of Mahanataka or Hanumanti Kavya.11 According to Satyendranath Sarmah the plot of Ram Bijay has been taken from Adikanda of Ramayana. Ram- Lakshmana's visit to Siddhasram with Biswamitra and then Ram's visit to Sita sayambar, breaking of Haradhanu, Parasuraama darpasurna and finally Rama's return to Ayodhya accompanied by Sita – Ram-Bijay excludes all the relevant subject matters of Ramayana except these inseparable incidents.12 Sankardeva developed the story of Ramayana in his own way. He has added some of the things that are not in original text and has arranged some of the contents in his own typical style.[13]

The main Character of Ram-Bijoy is Ramchandra. In this play Sriram. Ram, Ramchandra are used to mean the same person. Ram is the son of Dasaratha. He is a Kshyatriya that refers to gallantry. He is very humble and cool and steady. When Rishi Koushika told Ram about the beauty of Sita he was highly attracted to Sita : "Sitaaka rup sampati suniye Ramaka mane kinchita madana bigara upajala"- this truly reflects the nature of a normal human being. On the other hand his victory over the various demons, kings and the activities like the breaking of Haradhanu reflacts his bravery. The act of giving life to Parasuram shows his greatness.

Sankardeva has mentioned several times in Ram Bijay that Ramchandra is not a normal human being but an 'Avatari Purush' or the incarnation of God:

(a) **Through the dialogue of Suttradhara at the very beginning of the play:** "Suttra//Bho Bho Sabhasad Sadhujana : Je Jagataka Parama Ishwara Narayan Bhumiko Bharo Harana Nimitte Dasharatha Ghrihe Avatarala : Xohi Bhagawanta SriRamroope Uhi Sabha Madhye Pravesha Koyo Kahu Sita Bibaha Bihara Nrittya Parama Kautuke Karaba : Taahe Savadhane Dekhaha Sunaha//" (page-4)

(b) **Through the dialogue of Sita:** "Sita Bola//Aahe Sakhisava, Parama Abhaginika Ki Puchaha: Haamu Purava Janama Iswara Narayanaka Swami Ischa Kaya Aneka Janama Kaayo Klesha Koriye Bohuto Barixa Tapasya Koyolu Tadantara Akashbani Sunala : Aahe Kanya – Tuhu Uhi Janame Swamika Bheta Naahi Pawaba Aaworo Janama Sri Ram rupe Tuhaka Bibaha Korawaba : Iha Jani Hamu Agani Praveshi Prana Charala Aahe Sakhisava Xe Daibabani Biphala Bhela – Xe Sri Rama Swamika Charana Uhi Janama Bheta Nahi Pawalu" (page-7)

(c) **Through the dialogue of Rishi Biswamitra :** "Rishi Bola // Oye Dasharatha, Tuhu Ramaka Charitra Kisu Janoye Nahi : Yogabole Hamu Saba Janu : Uhi Ramachandra Parama Iswara Maha Harika Ansha Avatara, Asura Rakshasa Saba Sanghari Bhumika Bhara

Uddharava, Iha Jani Kisu Chinta Nahi Korobi: Satya Rakhi Satvare Rama Lakshmanaka Hamako Sange Pothawo." (Page-12)

(d) Through the dialogue of Parashurama : "Parashurama Bola // He Prabhu Sri Ram, Tuhu Parama Iswara, Hamu Tuhari Ansha, Iha Nojani Darpa Koyolu : Hamaro Dosha Maraxa Gosai." (page. 38)

The play starts with the glorification of Ram and salutation to Ram in the following way:

Dhrum – **Jaya Jagajivana Ram**
Koyolu Pori Paranam
Pada – **Jahe Guna Nama Muhe Gayi**
Papi Parama Pada Payo
Uhi Bhava Taapa Apaara
Jahe Smarane Koru Para
Ajagava Bhanjanakaari
Pawala Janaka Kumari
Nripa Xawa Chedala Baane
Krishna Kinkara Ehu Bhaane (page. 2)

Sankardeva says towards the end the play through the dialogue of Suttradhara in Sanskrit as:

Sloka – **SriRam Bijayannam Natankam Purnatangam**
Sri Krishnapadapadmasya Prasadena Sunischitam Suttra
Sri Krishna Pada Padma Prasadata Rama
Bijaya Naama Nataka Sampurna Bhela (page. 41)

Sankardeva admitted that it is through the blessings of Krishna that the plays could be completed. This expresses Sankardeva's faith in Bhagabata. In Sankardevas views 'Krishnastu Bhagaban swyam'. This is the decision of Bhagabata too. Murari is one of the synonyms for Krishna. In the last part of Ram-Bijay there is–

"Jaya Jaya Iswara Raghava Ram
Purala Jo Janeki Mana Kam
Jagajana Jivana Xohi Murari
Mukuti Mangala Karatu Tohari (page.4)

In this way Ram, Murari, Krishna refers to the form in Ram-Bijay. In addition to this Muktimangal bhatima ends with 'kara aba saba nara Hari Hari rol' and in between the play Sutradhara says, 'nirantare Hari bol Hari bol' and 'daki bola Rama Rama' – which glorifies the name of Hari.

Similarities of Kitan-Ghosa, Bargeet and Ram Bijay :

(a) Three of the types depict the greatness of Ram naam.
(b) Salvation is achieved through Ram naam – It has been mentioned in three of these types.
(c) These three types signify Ram naam and have been composed with the objective of preaching Naamdharma.

Conclusion

The following points have been put forward to conclude the discussion:

1. The two forms of Ram are there in the Kirtan-Ghosa, Bargeet and Ram Bijay.

   Ram: Name of God (Gunanaam) nirguna
   Name of the Avatar or the incarnation of God (Byaktirup) saguna

Again, the two forms of Ram mentioned above has been depicted through the following names –

Ram of Ram Bijay

Name of God (Gunanaam)	Name of the Avatar or the incarnation of God (Byaktirup)
Ram, Sri Ramchandra	Ram, Ramchandra, Sri Ram, Sri Ramchandra

Ram in Bargeet

Name of God (Gunanaam)	Name of the Avatar or the in carnation of God (Byaktirup)
Ram, SriRam	Ram, Raghaba, Raghupati

Ram in Kirtan-Ghosa

Name of God	Name of the Avatar or the in carnation of God (Byaktirup)
Ram, SriRam, Raghaba, Raghupati	SriRam, Raghaba, Raghunatha

2. The name of Ram is regarded as the greatest of all.
3. 'Ram' Pada is used as the name of the Supreme Lord in Kirtan-Ghosa and Bargeet.
4. The main character of Ram-Bijay play is Ram. He is the incarnation of the Lord. Therefore, Ram as incarnation of God has been used several times (considering the number of Pada).
5. The main theme of the three types is – Glorifying Ram as the name of the Supreme Lord.

6. Sankardeva's Kirtan-Ghosa, Bargeet and Ram-Bijay play depicts that Ram is used as synonym for Krishna, the Lord. In a sense both the names Ram and Krishna mean the same.
7. There is the need of further research on the depiction and use of Ram in the entire literature of Sankardeva.

References

1. Satyendra Nath Sarmah; Asomiya Sahityar Samikhyatmak Itibritwa, p. 132
2. "santa Sankardeve Gitar eksharan, Bhagabatar satsanga aru Sahasranaamar naam ei tinir ekatra samahar kari prabartan karile eksaran naamdharma." -Nagen Saikia; Bisaya Sankardeva, p.48
3. ibid, p.61
4. Bapchandra Mahanta; Sankardevar Darshan, p.230
5. ibid, p.239
6. Banikanta Kakati; Banikanta-Chayanika, p.101
7. ibid
8. ibid, p.103
9. Bapchandra Mahanta; Bargeet, p.90
10. Ankamala; p. 42
11. Maheswar Neog; Asamiya Sahityar Ruprekha, p.92
12. Satyendra Nath Sarmah; Asomiya Natya-Sahitya, p.59
13. Maheswar Neog; Asamiya Sahityar Ruprekha, p.93

Bibliography

Primary Source

1. **Kirttan-Ghosa Aru Naam-Ghosa :** Srimanta Sankardeva Sangha, Nagaon, 3rd edition, 1999
2. **Bargeet :** Bapchandra Mahanta (ed.), Student stores, Guwahati, 1992
3. **Ankamala :** Keshabanada Deva Goswami (ed.), Bonlata, Guwahati, 1988

Secondary Source

1. **Kakati, Banikanta :** Banikanta-Chayanika; Maheswar Neog (ed.), Sahitya Academy, New Delhi, 1998
2. **Neog, Maheswar :** Asamiya Sahityar Ruprekha, Chandra Prakash, Guwahati, 1995
3. **Mahanta, Bapchandra :** Sankardevar Darshan, Layers Book Stall, Guwahati, 1994
4. **Saikia, Nagen :** Bisaya Sankardeva, Kiran Prakashan, Dhemaji, 2008
5. **Sarmah, Satyendra Nath :** Asomiya Natya-Sahitya, Soumar Prakash, Guwahati, 2000
6. **... ...** : Asomiya Sahityar Samikhyatmak Itibritwa, Soumar printing & publishing limited, Guwahati, 1984

Chapter VII

Reflection of Indigenous Culture in Karbi and Khamti Ramayan

Prof. (Dr.) Jyotsna K.B. Rout

Karbis, linguistically belonging to Tibeto-Barman Group are the third largest tribe of Assam, reside mainly in Karbi-Anglong and Hamren districts of Assam. Their population stands at 4,06,000 as per 2001 census. A lyrical form of tale of Ramayan called 'Sabin Alun' is prevalent mostly in the Hamren district. Though the main theme of Ramayan is the basis of 'Sabin Alun', the socio-religious-geographical set up is suitably modified to suit the local tradition, beliefs and geography. Sita is known as Sinta Konwari, Dasrath as Dahram,

Meghnad as Meknad, Mahiravan as Muhiravan, Janaka as Bamanpo, Queen of Janak as Bamanpi, Surpanakha as Thes-mahadi, Hanuman as Uliman, Parsuram as Borpuram, the Creator as Hemfu, Sugriv as Hikring in Sabin Alun. Ayodhya is believed not as a city in Uttar Pradesh but a place in Karbi hills and Sita is portrayed as a Karbi Princess with expertise in weaving. Even she, like other Karbi-girls, carries Harlang (country-liquor) with rice, meat, fish etc. to her father who does jhum cultivation. Gandha Mardan hill, Ravan's Lanka etc. are identified with hills and town of Hamren and nearby district of Hojai.

The Khamtis are a part of great Shan or Tai or Thai race that migrated from upper Myanmar and settled in Tinsukia and Lakhimpur district of Assam and nearby Lohit district of Arunachal Pradesh. They follow Theravada school of Buddhism. According to 2011 census, their population stands at 14,031 out of which 12,925 live in Arunachal Pradesh and 1,106 in Assam.

The Khamti Ramayan in Tai Khamti language is known as

'Cao-alang-Lamang' (the story of Rama's incarnation) or Lik-Cao Lamang (the Ramayana Book). The manuscript is still preserved in the Buddha-Vihar of Narayanpur in Lakhimpur district.

Since the Khamtis are Buddhists, Cao Lamang (Sri Ram) is portrayed as a Bodhistva. Though the main theme of this Ramayan has great similarity with

Valmiki/Krittibas/Kandoli Ramayan, many chapters of above Ramayans are not incorporated in Khamti Ramayan e.g. killing of Tadaka, Khar-Dushan, Trishira, Kabandh etc. The salvation of Ahalya, search of Sita by the monkeys, role of Sampati are no where described in this Ramayan. The Adi-kanda, Lanka-kanda, Uttara-kanda of Valmiki Ramayan have great similarity with this Ramayan where as Ayodhya-kanda, Aranyak-kanda, Kishkinda-kanda, Sundara-kanda have some dis-similarity in Khamti Ramayan. The Khamti's beliefs and Buddhist traditions got profound reflection in the Khamti Ramayan.

In this paper a comparative study of the reflection of indigenous culture in both the Ramayans is done.

Chapter VIII

The Relevance of Ram in the Present Scenario of India

Kalpana Agarwal

'Ram' is closely associated with the lives of the folks of India. Since ancient times, 'Ram' has been in the daily life of Indian folks. He is everywhere. Ram is in the speeches of Indian folks,in their daily works, in their songs. Ram is in every cultural trait- Ram is "Maryada Purushuttam". The idealist view of life is associated with "Ram". Mahatma Gandhi dreamt of an ideal society (Ram Rajya) in India. The relevance of 'Ram' cannot be denied in this modern era. The major aim of the present study is to highlight the relevance of 'Ram' in various spheres and its necessity of scientific based study.

(Keywords : Relevance of Ram, Ram Rajya, Maryada Purushuttam)

Ram is closely associated with the lives of the folks of India, particularly folks belonging to Hindu religion. They utter the name of Ram very devotedly. He is everywhere. He is in their daily lives and in their works. Since ancient times, He has been an ideal figure for the Indian folks.

The folks consider him as God and an ideal man. As regards Ramayana, "Rama" means goodness and "ayana" means journey. Therefore "Ramayana" means journey to goodness. Ram is "Maryada purushuttam". Ram is the seventh Avatar of Lord Vishnu in Hinduism and a king of Ayodhya." As in the case of Krishna, here too, Rama is a historical Prince and perhaps also a tribal hero, who had been elevated to the position of a god and an incarnation of Visnu." (Sarma 63)

He was an avatar of the Lord but as a human being he suffered a lot. His life and journey may be considered as an example of perfect adherence to dharma inspite of the fact that he came across the harsh tests of time. He is regarded as " Purushuttam" i.e., peerless among men as he stuck to his propriety of conduct all through his life. Ram was an ideal son to his parents. It was for the sake of his father King Dasharath that Ram abandoned his claim to the throne and left for exile for a long period of fourteen years.

He was an ideal husband. Ram and Sita were deeply in love with each other. Theologically, they are the incarnations of Vishnu and Lakshmi respectively. He was a brother who loved his brothers truly and equally. As a king, he was responsible to be a role model for his subjects.

The study has been made on the basis of the following points :

Ram is Maryada Purushuttam

Ram is Maryada Purushuttam which means perfect man. His birth on this earth is considered to have occurred in order to destroy the evil forces. Ram is widely accepted to be a tribal hero of ancient India. It is on the basis of Ram's deeds that Valmiki wrote the great epic of Ramayana. It is believed that Ram lived in the Treta Yug.But historians are of the view that Ram was not particularly deified until the 11th century A.D. Tulsidas's version of the Sanskrit epic Ramayana into Ramcharitmanas. Greatly enhanced the popularity of Ram as a Hindu God. He was a paragon of virtues. He was indeed kind, affectionate, generous and considerate towards everyone.

After fourteen years of exile and killing of Ravan, Ram came back to Ayodhya. He was coronated as King of Ayodhya. King Ram's court had an efficient system of receiving feedback from the public. But the feedbacks were disturbing as they were about Sita. As per rule, Sita could not be accepted back as queen after staying with Ravan. Ram always respected the "Maryada" or existing tradition of his time.

Ram was truthful. His ideology of truthfulness has been a source of inspiration to everyone in India. Mahatma Gandhi was highly influenced by it. He was himself a person who followed the path of truthfulness. Mahatma Gandhi dreamt of building up India a Ram where people would follow Ram's ideologies. Mahatma Gandhi insisted on the building of a peaceful nation where people would follow non-violence. He uttered "Hey Ram". In a sense, he reminded himself of the ideologies of Ram.

Ram in the Day to Day Lives of Indian Folks

Indian folks, particularly the Hindus, perform their daily duties in the name of Ram. They find peace while they work in the name of Ram. They take the name of Ram in the following ways:

Uttering Ram Naam

Indian folks value "Ramayana" and utter the name "Ram" or " Ram naam". They feel Ram everywhere. They value him in their speeches, in their songs and in their day to day lives. Ram, the character of "Ramayana" is believed to be the seventh avatar of Lord Vishnu. It is believed that he existed during the Treta Yug. He was the incarnation of the Lord but the stories associated with his life reflect the hardships he had overcome through his life as a human being. People are attracted towards Ram and his suffering because such problems arise in a human being's life. The life of Ram reflect the reality a person has to face during his or her lifetime. A common man associates the stories of Ram with his own life. It is very common that a person in India particularly belonging to Hindu religion utter "Ram Naam" with utmost devotion. He or she finds peace of mind while uttering his name. Actually, "Ramayana" speaks of the true identity of a person. It reflects the real significance of a family and along with it the sanctity of the society. It teaches the significance of human values.

Naming a Person as Ram or With a Name That Starts with Ram

In India it is very common that people name a person as Ram, Ram Mohan, Ramprasad, Rambilas, Ramkrishna, Ramgopal, Ramratan, Ramsakhi, Ramdin and so on. A person is named as Ram or a name starting with Ram because" Ram Naam" is believed to be sacred and pure. It is expected that a person named in the name of Ram would be a good person. Parents expect their child would acquire all the ideal qualities of Ram while they name their child in the name of Ram.

Use of Ram Naam in Folk Songs

The name of Ram is used in folk songs. Instances may be cited of "Biyanaam" of Assam in India. A few of them are as follows :

(a) *"Dupine duxaari maahonire bari oi Ram taar maaje toruwa kodom Doiye pani tule Kanaye doliyai oi Ram toruwa kodomot uthi he Duroke pukhuri khonala pitadeu oi Ram bondhala senduri aali he….." (Goswami 20)*

(b) *" Ga dhui Aidewe borone xolale oi Ram haalodhi oti sorileSnanu korile bostrou pindhile oi Ram uri jau uri jau kore heGa dhui Aidewe Maakok xudhile oi Ram ki xaaj xolabo pai he……" (25)*

Mahatma Gandhi's Dream of a Ram Rajya

Mahatma Gandhi was the ardent devotee of Ram and as such he gave importance and valued Ram to a great extent. According to him, a nation like India may be built up to be a peaceful nation by following the non-violent ideologies. Then only a nation consisting of justice may be built up. Tolerance and patience are very significant in creating a peaceful atmosphere in a country. Violence can never solve problems. Rather it would increase chaos.The present day society needs to follow the Dharma that is contained in the epic Ramayana. There are several reasons behind this need. Most of the times, it is seen that chaos and troubles are created due to various factors. Instances are many. A student should follow his teacher or Guru but nowadays, students are seen to deviate from their duties towards their Guru or teacher. Corruption is very common everywhere. It is seen in the field of education, business and politics. Ram and Ravan are equally versed in all forms of knowledge. Valmiki depicts Ram as divine and Ravan as foolish. Ram converted all his knowledge into actions but Ravan was as opposed to Ram. Ram engaged himself in the welfare of every human being. He was in a way, master of all knowledge. So, people should try to be like Ram not like Ravan who was least concerned about the welfare of others. Today, in a materialistic world people behave like animals. They are least bothered about others. They are just busy with their power and worldly gains. People should not forget Ram and Ramayana. As regards Gandhiji's dream of building Ram Rajya, it is not seen today. People are seen to forget even Mahatma Gandhi and his ideologies.

One very significant point is that Gandhi ji paid heed on the unity among people belonging to different religions. He did not discriminate between Hindu, Muslim, Sikh, Isai. Rather he wanted a peaceful secular nation.

Ram's Sacrifice

Ram may be regarded as an example of upholding moral values in the society. Ram was sent to the exile for a long period of fourteen years while he was supposed to be coronated. He obeyed the order of his father. He did not refuse at all. Today, every human being hanker after power. But Rama did not crave for the throne. Rather, he obeyed what he was asked to do. He sacrificed for his father King Dasharath.

Conclusion

Since ancient times, the Indian folks have been singing the story of Ram.The story of "Ramayana" is very enchanting and interesting. People love to hear it again and again. It demonstrates that sincerity and devotion can lead to the formation of an ideal society. The story of Ram has been a great source of inspiration to Indian folks.

References

1. Bezbarooa, Lakshminath. Tattva-Katha.Sri Makhan Hazrika, on behalf of Banalata, Dibrugarh, Assam, 1999. Print.
2. Goswami, Dr. Praphulladatta. Bara Mahar Tera Git. Sahitya Akademi, 1993. Print.
3. Sarma, N.C. Folk elements in the Puranas. Department of Folklore Research, Gauhati University, 1997-98. Print. Vol. & No. 5 of Bulletin of the Department of Folklore Research.
4. Sarmah, Sri Satyendranath. Ramayanar Itibritta. Dr. Mahendra Bora, Dibrugarh University, Dibrugarh, 1984. Print.
5. Bakshi, Rajni. "Gandhi's Ram-Rajya" kiskikahani.openspaceindia.org

Chapter IX

Influence of Ramayana in Assamese Oral Literature

Lina Devi

The Ramayana is one of the great epics in Indian literature as well as literature of the world. The Hindu art, religion and cultural history have been primarily affected by this literary work of ancient India. The Ramayana has travelled through centuries and civilizations in the Indian origin and culture. Its influence has been on every living being not only in India, but also almost the whole of South-East Asia. The Great Indian values and heritage owes its existence to Valmiki's epic story. Even in today's generations, the basic human ethics and values can be traced out back to the Ramayana. Ramayana can answer all our questions and problems of our present life. The solutions to our problems lie in following the ideologies presented in the epic. In the field of Literature, many great writers have been influenced by Valmiki's Ramayana. Even the masterpieces by the great Kalidasa, was inspired from Ramayana. Prominent impacts of Ramayana in his works can be seen in 'Raghuvamsam'.

The Indian literature is greatly influenced by this holy epic. It's influence in Assamese literature is also remarkable. Every language has their own literature, both in written as well as oral forms. Similarly, the Assamese language also has written and oral forms in abundance.

Oral literature may be called 'verbal art' or 'expressive' literature. Oral literature are spoken, sung and voiced forms of traditional utterances. It includes folk songs, proverbs, tales etc. These folk songs, tales etc are still continuing amongst people, generation after generation in oral forms, in spite of the pressing influence of the modern civilization. There are various types of literature in oral form which have enriched the field of Assamese literature. In the Assamese literature, the popularity of Ramayana is above of all. Rama centric stories are always heart touching for everyone. Hence, a huge number of Assamese songs and tales are directly influenced by the epic Ramayana. Lokageet, proverbs, folk tales etc are some prominent example of oral literature which are influenced by Ramayana. Among these example lokageet is said to be the most important and emotionally attached to the social life of Assamese culture. These all will elaborately be discussed in this paper.

Oral Literature of Assam

Oral tradition, or oral lore, is a form of human communication where in knowledge, art, ideas and cultural material is received, preserved and transmitted orally from one generation to another. The transmission is through speech or song and may include folktales, chants, prose or verses. In this way, it is possible for a society to transmit oral history, oral literature, oral law and other knowledge across generations without a writing system, or in parallel to a writing system. Indian religions such as Buddhism, Hinduism and Jainism have used an oral tradition, in parallel to a writing system, to transmit their canonical scriptures, secular knowledge such as Sushruta Samhita, hymns and mythologies from one generation to the next.

Oral literature can be said as pre-literate societies that have no written literature, but may possess rich and varied oral traditions such as folk epics, folklore, proverbs and folksong which effectively constitute an oral literature. When these are collected and published by scholars such as folklorists and paremiographers, than it known as oral literature.

This oral literature is also found in Assamese culture. Here, influence of Ramayana is often seen not only in oral literature, it influences all the field of a society. Ethical value is an important factor of Ramayana which can refine a society. Going through the topic of this paper, now going to discuss about Ramayana's influence in oral literature which includes folk song, folk tales, proverbs etc.

Ramayana's influence in oral Literature

(i) Folk Song

The treasury of Assamese folk songs are very rich. It included biya nam, diha nam, bihu nam, aai nam, dhai nam, oja pali etc. The influence of Ramayana is seen in some of these folk songs.

A. Biyanaam

Marriage is one of the memorable occasion of one's life. It is a common social phenomenon of human being. The folk songs of the Assamese is said to be rich in respect of marriage songs. Generally, these songs have been sing since early periods according to their traditional customs. These are performed by womenfolk in various ritualistic functions of Assamese marriage. Lyrics of these marriage songs usually contain descriptions of the life of the bride her close relationship with the family members especially with the brothers, sisters, mother and the father. The life of the bride, in the village, where she is born and brought up is also beautifully narrated in these marriage songs. Sometimes it is seen that the legendary characters of popular legends like Krishna-Rukmini, Usha-Aniruddha, Arjun-Subhadra etc. also describes to compare the couple in Assamese Biya naam. Some marriage folk songs that are influenced by Ramayana are as follows –

Ram Krishna hori muroi Zoi Jamunaloi jaow
Ram Krishna ulahor rohini Ram Krishna doiboki sundori
Hori muroi kiyo koriso hela//[1]

There are many numbers of Biya naam[2] that are influenced by Ramayana.

In these folk songs, they exhort the bride and groom to utter the name of Radha or Rukmoni and Lord Rama. The language of the marriage song is very simple but meaningful. The bride is traditionally bathed and decorated with new dresses and ornaments. The womenfolk of the bride's side express the beauty of bride through marriage folk songs.

Bihunaam

Bihu is the chief festival of Assam. Hence, bihu songs are the integral part of the folk songs. These songs also give us a picture of the social and domestic life of people. Human being is a social animal. Without society human beings cannot live in the world. They are influenced by society in every way. The social life of the people of Assam is reflected very clearly. Ramayana is that epic which is reflected in all the fields including bihu songs. In the following songs, the utterance Rama is seen.

Krishnai murote bokul phul epahi,
Niyor pai mukoli hol O! Gobindai ram

The meaning of the song is that on the head of the Lord Krishna there is a piece of Bokul flower, It is blooming with dew,O! Lord Ram

Another bihu song[3] is found that is influenced by Ramayana.

Rongpuror husori, Ahisu susori,
Bihu mariboloi Jaow bol, Gobindoi ram

It means that Husori dance team of Rongpur, Coming to crawl
Lets' go for Bihu dance O! Lord Ram.

Generally, the Husori is performed by the male and there is no place for woman.

Dihanaam

Dihanaam is a type of congregational prayer sung by women in Assam, in praise of the gods. Instruments like the Negera, taal, khol and hand clapping is used in it. Here are two distinct parts of the lyrics of naams- the first part is diha and the rest is Pada. Diha is continuously sung as chorus and the main singer sings the Pada. Some myth of Ramayana's are also sang by them. Diha is that where only the gist of naam is depicted. On the other hand, Pada is the description of gist. The aim of this Diha Naam is to pray to god and to inform the common people about the myth of Rama. In the book of Dihanaam, a huge number of Naams are found where Rama is eulogised. For Example -

Diha - **Puje Rame abhayar carane, dasanan badh hetu**
akala bodhane, puje abhayar carane

Pad - **Sandi path kari rame karila utsav**
geet vadya jayadhvani kare kapisav
mahanande naase aru devi gun gaai
devir archane surjya astachale jai

In the above naam Rama's worship to Durga is delineated. The part of Diha imply that Rama offer prayer in the feet of Durga, to kill dasanana i.e. Ravana. Pada denotes that after having sandi path, Rama celebrated with a great pleasure. So, songs instruments and victory sounds (jayadhvani) are used. Danced with pleasure and worshipped devi the whole day. In this context, there are found. Many diha naam.

(ii) Incantation

The incantation is an integral part of Assamese folk literature. An incantation is a charm or spell created using and it may take place during a ritual, either a hymn or prayer, and may invoke or praise a deity. The incantations are oldest part of folk literature. In ancient Assam (Kamrup) it was very much popular among the people. Women also take part in incantation literature. The main principle of incantation is to keep secret but later it comes out mouth to mouth among the peoples. It is not easy to find out when the incantation started. Since ancient time, the incantation has been maintained in Assamese society.On the other hand, the incantation is not related to festivals in Assamese society. Of course, the Assamese people are maintaining it, only for preventing various types of diseases and evil powers. Here also found the Ramayana's influence. The following incantation is sung in Assamese society to make dry the burning place of human body that is influenced by Ramayana–

Rame phalile khori, Laxmane jolale zui
Sitai Pani Dhali thake Zene tene hoi...
Longkar Agni humontoi khai Mukhor agni, mukhe numai[6]

It means Ram bring out fire wood Laxman burned it,Sita pouring water on the fire, Honuman eat the fire of Lanka and the mouth eats the fire.

The incantations are oldest part of folk literature. In ancient Assam (Kamrup) it was very much popular among the people. Women also take part in incantation literature. The main principle of incantation is to keep secret but later it comes out mouth to mouth among the peoples. It is not easy to find out when the incantation was started.

(iii) Folk Tales

Assamese oral literatures are very rich in folk tales. These tales are described mostly in narrative styles. Tales are still continuing mostly amongst the illiterate sections of the society, generation after generation in oral form. The folk tales do not have a specific structure or foundation. The person by his own limitation and capacity, describes those tales. Different folk tales depict different stages of the society and its people. The folk tales exposes the superstitious beliefs, likings and disliking, anger etc, prevailing in the community, which are skillfully narrated. Incidentally, it also focuses indirectly to the moral ideals and truthfulness. Thus, some myth of great epic Ramayana is used to give the knowledge of good or bad. It depicts the duties of relationship, portraying ideal characters like the ideal father, the ideal servant, the ideal brother, the ideal wife. Therefore the tale of Ramayana is used to give the proper knowledge to children. It can give a positive environment.

(iv) Proverbs

A proverb is a short saying that conveys commonly held ideas in a certain culture. It can express a prevalent moral or a generally accepted observation about life, based on experience. They are all part of the oral tradition of a linguistic or cultural group. Proverbs must be vivid and they must have the quality that they can be easily remembered. Because proverbs are usually spoken and not written, they relate to everyday wisdom people want to convey in speech. Proverbs are usually illustrated with homely imagery using household objects, farm animals, pets, and events of daily life. Many proverbs are based on customs that are obsolete. The Assamese terms like yojona or Yojana as well as prabacan and patantar are used to suggest the sense of the proverb. A large number of Assamese proverb which are based on the theme of Ramayana are able to give us a fair knowledge of the different situations and episodes of the great epic. Such proverbs are given below–

ram nau upojotei ramayana - this means before Rama takes birth, the Ramayana comes out.

sei ramo nai sei ayodhyao nai - it means that Rama is no more, that Ayodhya is no more.

Such influence of Ramayana is vividly reflected in every form of oral literature.

Conclusion

From the above discussion it is found that all the forms of Assamese oral literature is greatly influenced by the epic Ramayana. It is the storehouse of all kinds of knowledge. In the field of literature, Ramayana is the root of all. As it is regarded as adikavya, so it is obvious to see the impact of this great epic in later literature. The treasury of Assamese oral literature is very rich. Here found many kind of forms like folk songs, incantation, tales, proverbs etc and Ramayana's influence on this literature is also discussed above. There are many form of oral literatures are left to discuss, because it is not possible to include all of those. But Ramayana's influence is verily acceptable. The Ramayana is not just an epic or a tale, but also an educational medium to demonstrate the importance of values such as loving and respecting family, keeping promises, protecting the weak and so on. By using the Magnum Opus of Hindu mythology, the Ramayana as a medium, one can teach their children many life-skills and ethics. In the end, I would like to cite the following verse wishing long life of Ramayana

Yavat sthasyanti girayah saritacsa mahitale
tavad ramayanakatha lokesu prasarisyati

উদ্যোগত আৰু
এপ্ৰিল

Chapter X

The Relevance of Ram-kathaa in the Present Scenario

Partibha Tomar

Sauryam tejo dhritirdaksham yuddhe chaapyapalayanam
Daanamishvarabhavashca kshatram karma svabhaavajam

Heroism, majesty, firmness, diligence and dauntlessness in battle, bestowing gifts, and lordliness-all these constitute the natural duty of a Kshatriya.

The main source of Ram-kathaa is Valmiki Ramayana. Vedic civilization, popularly known as Hindu civilization is the oldest civilization when the Western world was reeling under ignorance and undeveloped even the name of Christ and Prophet Mohammed were unknown. The main three things of Vedic religion are- sacrifice, austerities and hermitage. The main objective of these are the achievement of dharma, artha, kama, and moksha. The epic period (The period of Ramayana and Mahabharata and Bhagavat Mahapurana) is rightly called as the extension of Vedic culture. Valmiki Ramayana, Mahabharata and Bhagvat Purana, the three works of Sanskrit literature influenced Indian mind through ages and still its influence is witnessed in every sphere of Indian life. Though scholars differ about the period of Valmiki Ramayana, its present volume has many editions and sub-editions.

Following this great epic, many great works were written in many languages worldwide though some changes have appeared according to the beliefs, customs and traditions of the concerned land. The main story behind the epic was the quest of Rishi Valmiki to sage Narada to narrate the story of a person of sublime virtues by listening or following the ideal of which people of Kalyug would attain liberation.

> The following verses of Srimad Vamiki Ramayana as mentioned in Book 1 of Balakanda Charitren cha koyuktaha sarvabhuteshu ko hitaha...
>
> Who can possibly be full of virtues in this world at present? Nay, who is possessed of prowess and knows what is right? Who is conscious

of services done, truthful of speech and firm of resolve? (2) Who is possessed of right conduct and who is friendly to all living beings? Who is a man of knowledge? Nay, who is powerful and who has a singularly loveable appearance? (3) Who has subdued his self? Who has conquered anger? Who is possessed of splendor and who is above fault finding, and whom do the very gods dread when his wrath has been (apparently) provoked in battle?

Listening to these words of Narada, Vamiki composed the beautiful epic of Ramayana. Maharishi Valmiki narrates the story of Shri Rama, the seventh avatar of Vishnu, and the 64th ruler of the Suryavansh dynasty of Iksvaku lineage.

Yada yada hi dharmasya glanirbhavati bharata
Abhyuthanamadharmasya tadatmanam srijamyaham
Paritranaya sadhnaam vinashay cha dushkritam
Dharmasansthapanarthay sambhabami yuge yuge

Arjuna, whenever righteousness is on the decline, unrighteousness is in the ascendant, then I body Myself forth. For the protection of the virtuous, for the extirpation of evil-doers, and for establishing Dharma (righteousness) on a firm footing, I manifest Myself from age to age.

There are three main purposes of incarnation of Lord Vishnu. These are: the establishment of dharma (righteousness) on a firm footing, the protection of the virtuous and extirpation of evil-doers.

People of divine and demonic nature always existed on the earth. By the extirpation of evil-doers good people can be saved. Only then Dharma can be established. Lord Rama, a Kshatriya prince is full of Kshatriya qualities as laid by scriptures and full of sublime and divine virtues. Rama represents the Supreme Personality of Godhead : Fearlessness; purification of one's existence; cultivation of spiritual knowledge; charity; self-control; performance of sacrifice; study of the Vedas; austerity; simplicity; nonviolence; truthfulness; freedom from anger; renunciation; tranquility; aversion to faultfinding; compassion for all living entities; freedom from covetousness; gentleness; modesty; steady determination; vigor; forgiveness; fortitude; cleanliness; and freedom from envy and from the passion for honor -- these transcendental qualities belong to godly men endowed with divine nature.

Pride, arrogance, conceit, anger, harshness and ignorance -- these qualities belong to those of demoniac nature. The transcendental qualities are conducive to liberation, whereas the demoniac qualities make for bondage. In this world there are two kinds of created beings. One is called the divine and the other demoniac. Those who are demoniac do not know what is to be done and what is not to be done. Neither cleanliness nor proper behavior nor truth is found in them. Bharata is considered the land of religion or righteousness. In other countries God sends his messengers or son while in Bharatabhumi He takes the form of incarnation from time to time to lead the people towards the path of righteousness, piety and knowledge. Lord Buddha, ninth incarnation of Vishnu, did not show reverence to Vedic practices of sacrifice and also criticized Varnashram and other rules laid down by Vedic scriptures. The reason behind Buddhist philosophy was to liberate people from the clutches of excessive sacrifices and drinking which were prevalent during the time of Lord Buddha. There are people who are qualified for Yajna and some are not. Unqualified people for the study of Vedas and Vedic practices were attracted towards Buddhism. Thus he saved Vedic religion only for qualified people to follow and did a great justice to save humanity. For Raajsuya Yajna only a Kshatriya is qualified to perform and king's seat is higher than the priest's. Vajpaye Yajna is meant for Brahmins only. No other religion in the world has given so high place to a person of other religion. This was the negative approach to dissuade unqualified people to perform Yajna. When this task was accomplished, again Shankaracharya established the Vedic religion through positive approach.

Ram Rajya is the best example of good governance based on Dharma. From Plato to Aristotle, all have given the details of an ideal state and how it should be governed. Forgetting our own scriptures we tend to look at them which has led to no proper solution. Ramayana gives the detailed description of how an ideal state should be. How should people be governed? How should the ministers be? It can serve as the best example of statecraft. Valmiki Ramayana's Canto 6 and 7,Part 1,gives the description of the city of Ayodhya and the prosperity of its inhabitants during the reign of King Dasaratha and the virtue and the upright conduct of the eight ministers of Emperor Dasaratha which continued during the period of Lord Rama, is the best example of statecraft.

We often hear the term Ram Rajya. What is Ram Rajya? It is an epitome of good governance where Praja is everything for a true leader. Lord Rama, popularly known as Maryada Purushottam (ideal human being) is the perfect example of truthfulness, loyalty, contentment, integrity, humility in power and cool amidst the adversities define his universality of righteousness. The karma of a person decides his fate depending on the situation which may be socially or culturally determined.

Dharma was the basic principle for which Lord Rama left everything. The popular idiom :

Raghukul riti sada chali aayi
pran jaye par vachan na jaye

was lived up by Rama. For the protection of the vachan (promise) given by King Dasaratha to his wife Kaikei which even led to the death of Dasaratha and Rama had to go to exile for fourteen years, shows the true dedication of the words of Iksvaku lineage.

Jean Atticus Finch while explaining democracy in Harper Lee's To Kill a Mocking Bird (1989) says –" Equal rights to all, special privileges to none." We have often read in stories and history books that a king gives orders expecting others to act while in Ramayana it is Lord Rama who takes no special privilege and lives the life of an ordinary man. He is an epitome of truth. Untouched by desire, anger and greed he leads dispassionately yet for the cause.

Rama gives quality advice to Bharata when he counsels on the different facets of good governance which is the key to effective governance. Placing Bharata on his lap, Shri Rama gives instruction in judicature under the pretext of inquiring after the welfare of his father and others in Canto C, Part1 of Ayodyakanda.

On the death of Ravana (the king of ogres) his chief queen, Mandodari, while lamenting, held Ravana responsible for the destruction and devastation of Lanka. She said:

> **When the time (for retribution) comes, O husband, the doer assuredly reaps the fruit of his sinful deed: there is no doubt about it. The doer of a blessed act gathers happiness, while the perpetrator of a sinful act reaps misery. While Vibhisana has attained happiness you have met with such an evil destiny.**

Lord Hanuman was wonderstruck to behold the splendor and glory of Ravana and believes that he could even rule heaven but for his gross unrighteousness, he was dragged down. Hanuman said to Ravana:

> **The fruit of virtue (practiced by you in the past) has already been attained (and enjoyed) by you; there is no doubt about it. You will reap the fruit of unrighteousness (in the shape of abduction and detention of Sita) too very soon. Recalling the extermination of the ogres of Janasthana as well as the destruction of Vali as also the alliance of Shri Rama with Sugriva,ponder over your own interest.**

Lord Rama killed Ravana but he did not annex his empire and installed Vibhishana on the throne of Lanka. He even did not enter Lanka following the words of his father. After killing Vali, Sugriv was given the throne, and son of Vali, named Angad was installed as prince regent. There were many other feudal chiefs like Nishadaraaj Guha and others who were under Lord Rama. He gave the Vedic or Aryan constitution to rule the people and never interfered with their social customs, traditions and practices. Still it was called Ram Rajya and a role model to rule. We never hear, even feudal chiefs deviated from their duties and did injustice to anyone.

In present day democracy we find many loopholes or defects. We have given voting right to eighteen years youth. Vedic code of conduct gives much importance to purity of heart then comes the rule. But in today's democracy only attaining eighteen years of age is sufficient to cast their vote and to shoulder any responsibility of administration. No importance is given to the purity of self. Vedic scriptures give the guidelines to rule and govern.

Hey eyachakshasa mitrasuryaha (etc) vayam swarajye aa yatemahi

The persons qualified to protect and rule should possess-

(a) broad outlook and farsightedness and be free from evil nature

(b) maintain friendly relation with all people and should not envy anyone

(c) they should be full of wisdom and possess accurate knowledge of governance.

Contrary to all these qualities, people with narrow outlook, bear enimosity and ill feeling towards others and full of ignorance are unqualified to rule.

To achieve the objects of welfare state it is imperative that governance should be given to only upright and good people. Selfish and wise people like Ravana will bring decay, despondency, desolation, death and overall destruction of the empire. Rama was the true Kshatriya leader who kept the welfare of his people above all caste, colour, creed and religion, and did not hesitate for any kind of sacrifice which are beyond the understanding of the modern mind of the mere imitators of the Western culture. Ravana, on the other hand, is referred as Lok-kantaka (the thorn of three worlds) and the possessor of demoniac qualities.UNO and other world democracies or kingship should follow the example of Ram Rajya to sustain peace and prosperity.

Ram-kathaa is the best example of Sanatan Dharma or Vedic religion as described in Vedas, Upanishads and other religious scriptures. Manusmriti tells us the ten different qualities of dharma which are:

> Patience (dhriti), forgiveness (kshama), piety or self control (dama), honesty (asteya), sanctity (shauch), control of senses (indraiya-nigrah), reason (dhi), knowledge or learning (vidya), truthfulness (satya) and absence of anger (krodha). Manu further writes, "Non-violence, truth,

non-coveting, purity of body and mind, control of senses are the essence of dharma".

The meaning of dharma is different from the word religion. In Hinduism, dharma has broad meaning and controls the every sphere of mankind. Bhagavadgita says:

Sarva dharman parityajya mam ekam saranam vrajya
Aham tva sarvapapebhyo mokshayisyami ma suchaha
Abandoning dependence on all duties (dharma),
take refuge in Me, alone. I shall liberate you from all your sins; therefore grieve not.

Here dharma means "the universal Spritual Truths that maintain balance in the world. Without that, imbalance and deterioration will surely follow." Varnashrama dharma laid certain duties for four varnas- Brahmana, Kshatriya, Vaishya and Shudra. They are:

Tranquility, restraint, austerity, purity, patience, integrity, knowledge, wisdom, and belief in a hereafter—these are the intrinsic qualities of work for Brahmins. Valor, strength, fortitude, skill in weaponry, resolve never to retreat from battle, large-heartedness in charity, and leadership abilities, these are the natural qualities of work for Kshatriyas. Agriculture, dairy farming, and commerce are the natural works for those with the qualities of Vaishyas. Serving through work is the natural duty for those with the qualities of Shudras.

Lord Rama followed the duties of a Kshatriya king sincerely and honestly from childhood to Saket-gaman (last time). He strictly followed the duties and code of conduct accordingly. He never told lies and kept his promise at all costs without taking wrong course. He promised Sugriv to kill Vali and did so. Rama says to Sugriv:

Listen, Sugriv: I will kill Vali with a single arrow. His life will not be saved even if he takes refuge with Brahma or Rudra. One would incur great sin by the very sight of those who are not distressed to see the suffering of a friend. A man should regard his own mountain-like troubles as far as of no more account than a mere grain of sand, while the troubles of a friend should appear to him like Mount Sumeru, though really they may be trifling as a grain of sand. Those fools who are not of such a temperament presume in vain to make friends with anyone. A friend should restrain his companion from the evil path and lead him on the path of virtue; he should proclaim the latter's good points and cover his faults.

What he said to Jatayu, he fulfilled his promise by exterminating evil-doer ogres. He further says:

> But on reaching there, my loved one, tell not my father about Sita's abduction. If I am no other than Rama the ten-headed Ravana alongwith his whole family will go and himself will say everything to him.

He promised to sages to extirpate ogres and that promise he fulfilled. Rama said to rishis:

> With uplifted arms Shri Rama took a vow to rid the earth of demons. Then he gladdened all the hermits by visiting their hermitages.

Kshatriya dharyate chapo nart shabdo bhavet

Using bow and arrow by a Kshatriya is only fruitful when he is capable of subduing evil-doers and protecting the destitute and helpless.

Ramo dwirnabhi bhasate

Rama never speaks in two ways. At all costs he kept his words. Keeping the words of his father he went to exile leaving the throne of Ayodhya for fourteen years and did not return from Chitrakoot although everyone wanted him to return, including Kaikei.

The four goals to achieve Purusartha chatustha is the supreme duty of a human being- Dharma, artha, kama, moksha.. Artha is the second Purusartha. As a Kshatriya king Rama did not levy undue tax.He collected the taxes as per the Vedas. Welfare of the subject is of prime importance to him. He never coveted others' property or land. When Laxmana made proposal to stay in Lanka after the death of Ravana, he said:

api svarnamayi lankaa na me lakshmana rochate
jananii janmabhumishca swargaadapi gariiyasi

Lakshman, Even though (Api) Lanka is full of gold (Swarna Mayi),
it doesn't give me happiness (Na may Rochate).

Mother (janani) and motherland (Janmabhoomi) are much higher and glorious than
(Gareeyasi) heaven (Swarga).

He never allowed administrative officers to exploit his subjects or do any kind of atrocities or injustice. His motto was :

Jasu raaj priya praja dukhari
So nrip awasi narak adhikari

Religion is the root of the welfare state: the righteousness of the people and the rulers. In Ram's monarchy we see the welfare of the people-power. Ram presents the ideal of the welfare ruler in front of us. The ideal ruler or government is the one who provides happiness to the people.

In our country taxes are levied unjustfully, people are treaded under the feet of administrative officers, justice is denied to common man as it is very expensive. There is no safety and security of life and property of common men, children, women and poor people are subject to various atrocities. The life of flora and fauna is at stake. Unbridled greed of leaders, administrators, judges, press have made the life of people miserable. Should all these learn to serve people following Ram-kathaa?

Kama or conjugal life is the third Purusartha. Lord Rama's father, King Dasaratha had three queens, Rama married Sita and he is the best example of monogamy. He outrightly rejected the practice of polygamy which was prevalent among Kshatriya class during those days. The following verse from Bhagavadgita clearly indicates that conjugal relations should be maintained as per the guidelines of the scriptures. Rama, his brothers and his subjects followed the example of Rama,

> Every husband was pledged to the vow of monogamy and the wives too were devoted to their husband in thought, word and deed.

Lord Krishna says in Bhagavadgita that I am cupid which is not opposite to dharma.

Dharmartha aviruddho kamo asmi

Liberation of soul from bondage of life and transitory world is the ultimate goal of mankind. Rama's life and personality was so inspiring that he attained this object with all his subjects. This type of mass liberation from the bondage has never been heard before. It was only possible because Rama led a life of piety, righteousness and purity of words, deeds and actions. He never deviated from the path of divine nature.

Rama's life and deeds are the best examples of national unity and integrity. Starting from the Vedic age the seeds of nationality and bond of human brotherhood existed in the scriptures. Rama's empire serves as a model to our democracy. His people were true to him. During his reign public unrest and dessention were not heard of. He maintained cordial relations with different tribes and communities which will serve as a role model to our present democracy.

Rama is the embodiment of sublime values. Humanity has never known such an illustrious, heroic personality of determination and unfailing denotion. Sage Valmiki has given detailed description of Rama's charismatic character which ever descended on earth. Lord Rama maintained cordial relations with all. His entire life is full of love and sacrifice for all. He is the best example as a son who went to exile to keep the words of his father. His preceptor and guru, his younger brother, Bharata, all three mothers including Kaikei, rishi Javali, his ministers and people, King Janaka and other relatives could not bring him back to Ayodhya. He returned to Ayodhya only after fourteen years when the time of Vanavasa was over. He treated all the mothers equally, even paid more reverence to Kaikei for sending him to exile so he could accomplish the task of his birth. He served as the best example of friendship to Sugriv, Nishadraj Guha and Vibhisana, and every soldier who fought with him was treated as a friend by Rama. While introducing all monkeys and bears to Guru Vasistha, he says :

E saba sakha sunahu muni mere,
bhae samara sagara kaha bere.
Mama hita lagi janma inha hare,
bharatahu te mohi adhika pyare.

(Turning to the sage) Listen, holy Sir: all these my Comrades proves as so many barks in taking Me across the ocean of the battle. They staked their life for My cause: they are endearing to Me even more than Bharata.

In the same way he addressed Nishadraj.

Tumha mama sakha bharataha sama bhrata,
sada rahehu pura avata jata

> You are My friend and friend as much as Bharata; you must continue to visit Ayodhya now and then.

He also addressed to His comrades as friends when he asked them to leave Ayodhya for their own abode.

Ab griha jahu sakha saba bhajehu mohi driha nema,
Sada sarbagata sarbahita jani karehu ati prema

> Now, My comrades, return to your homes all of you, and, worship Me with steadfast regularity. Knowing Me always as omnipresent and friendly to all, love Me most dearly.

When Rama made friendship with Sugriv, his words are a code of conduct for friendship. In today's world people make friends with their selfish motives. True friends are a rarity. Rama's friendship with Sugriv and Vibhisana served the basic purpose of extermination and extirpation of Ravana with his entire army of ogres. Good friends are a boon to accomplish the worldly gain.

Lord Rama and Ram-kathaa showed the way to lead a pure and purposeful life amidst adversities. It has inspired human mind across the globe, innumerable works has been written and still being written in different countries in different languages. To say something about Lord Rama and Ram-kathaa for me is showing a candle to the sun, the biggest source of energy and light. Keeping in mind my little knowledge and my limit of intellectual pursuits, I conclude with the two shlokas of Raghuvansham, Sarga1, by the great Sanskrit poet, Kalidasa.

Where the dynasty originated from Sun where the meagre intellect of mine with an intellect yet to be edified, am I inanely wishing to go across this unnavigable ocean called the solar dynasty by a small barque called my ersatz education? [2]

Or else, my course in depicting this dynasty might as well be easy through the idiomatic gateway already crafted by the earlier poets, like a diamond boreholed by a diamond-edged tool for an easy passage of thread. [4]

A Sanskrit poet rightly said till when mountains and rivers exist on earth, Ram-kathaa will follow upto eternity.

Jai Shri Rama.

Works Cited

1. Ved-kathank, Gitapress. Gorakhpur: Gitapress. 2015:534.
2. Upadhyay, Acharya Baldev. History of Sanskrit Literature. Varanasi: Sarda Mandir Publication. 1968:74-76.
3. Khemka, Radheshyam. Vedic Sukta Sangraha, Gorakhpur: Gitapress.2013:206.
4. Vivek Churamani. Gorakhpur: Gitapress. 2014:7.
5. Srimad Bhagavadgita. Vol1&2, Gorakhpur: Gitapress. 2012:469,1943-1945,1697-1710.
6. Upanishad-anka. Gorakhpur: Gitapress. 2014:564.
7. Manasa-piyush Gorakhpur: Gitapress. 2008:162-180.
8. Sadhak Sudha Sindhu Gorakhpur: Gitapress.
9. Shri Vishnu Purana, tr.Muni Lal Gupt, Gorakhpur: Gitapress. 2003: 175.
10. Dwivedi, Acharya Hazari Prasad. Bhasha Sahitya aur Desh. New Delhi: Bharati Gyanpeeth Prakashan.2nd edition, 1995:148.
11. Swami Prabhupada. Bhagavadgita as it is. Italy: Bhakti Vedanta Book Trust, 1972: 66-68.
12. Paatanjali Yogpradeep, Swami Somteertha Maharaja. Gorakhpur: Gitapress. 2015:406.
13. Suryanka. Gorakhpur: Gitapress.2014:440.
14. Shiv-strota Ratnakar. ed. Radheshyam Khemka. Gorakhpur : Gitapress. 2014:46.
15. Krativasi Ramayana. Gorakhpur: Gitapress. 6th reprint. 2013: 17.
16. Pathak, Pramod, Singh, Saumya and Ankita Anshul." Modern Management Lessons from Ramayana." SMS 9. No.1 (March 2016- August 2016): 51-57.
17. Hari, D.K. "Is Rama just a myth or really a Historical Figure?" vibsworldonline. Web.
18. Knapp, Stephen. "A Clarion Call to Save Your Culture, Before it's too late." http://stephen-knapp.com. 4May 2009.Web.
19. Knapp, Stephen. "Hindus Must Stand Strong for Dharma." http://stephen- knapp.com/lord_rama_or_fiction.htm. 28 March 2010. Web.
20. "Historicity of the Era of Lord Rama and Shri Krishna." www.serveveda.org/documents. pdf. 2-20. Web.
21. Srimad Valmiki Ramayana. Gorakhpur: Gitapress. Part 1& 2. 2014: 499-500, 168-173,624-686.
22. Srimad Bhagavad Mahapurana. Gorakhpur: Gitapress. Vol.1 & 2. 2012:60.
23. Tulsidas. Ramacharitamanas. Gorakhpur: Gitapress. 2014: 806-809.
24. Adhyatma Ramayana, tr,Gupt, Muni Lal. Gorakhpur: Gitapress. 2016: 344.

Chapter XI

Reflection of Ramakatha in Bharigaan

Rupanjoli Hazarika

Rama is the hero of Ramayana written by Balmiki. He was the son of Dasharatha and Kasaulya.Rama was sent to exile on the day of his proposed coronation ceremony by the plotting of his step mother Kaikeyi. He was virtuous, pious and popular among the people. Rama is considered as an incarnation of God. In fourteen years exile, his wife Sita was abducted by Ravana, king of Lanka. To rescue Sita, Rama had to engage in fight with Ravana. Finally with help of Sugriva, he rescued Sita and backed to Ayodhya. The iconic character of Rama had an impact on the people irrespective of time space or geographical region. The literature all over the world embraced Rama as an iconic character. Indian regional literatures also depicted story of Rama on their own. Of course, the stories got varied elements as the indigenous elements were added to this story. It has tremendously influenced the social life of the people inherent in Indian culture. Han is of the opinion that the influence of Ramayana is observed on relationship too.

> It (the Ramayana) is not only a literary treasure but also a source of ennobling influence on the relationships of men as parents and children, husbands and wives, brothers and sisters, relations and friends, teachers and pupils, and rulers and the ruled. (qtd. in Iyengar introduction I)

North east India has got so many tribal groups with their distinct literatures, cultures, dialects and languages. Pati Rabhas are one of the five sections of Rabhas. Mr Damant observed that-

> the Pati Rabhas have become to a great extent Hinduised and have abandoned their own language for Assamese; the reminder still preserve their own customs and language to a greater or less extent. (qtd. in Grierson 1: 357)

Bharigaan is a traditional folk theatre current in South Kamrup and Goalpara districts, more or less confined to the Pati-Rabhas. The subject matter of this folk theatre is mainly inspired by the Ramayana story apart from the 'Mahabharata' and 'Puranas', The Bharigaan troupe consists of a Mul (principal singer) and Palis (assistants) It reflects the folk lives of the Rabha people keeping in mind the Rama tradition influence upon the Indian culture. Moreover, Bharigaan has got very much impact on the common people as a source of entertainment in the form of folk theatre. My paper is an attempt to bring out the elements of popularity of Bharigaan amongst the Pati-Rabhas. It is also an attempt to find out the present techniques used in this performance along with possibilities of sustainability of the folk theatre in an age of market driven economy.

Objectives

(a) to bring forth various elements of Bharigaan as a folk theatre.

(b) to highlight Ramakatha depicted in Bharigaan

(c) to encourage research work on Bharigaan by highlighting its various aspects.

(d) to look into the prospects of providing a platform to the performers of Bharigaan.

The study is based on both primary and secondary data. The field data has been collected from Bharigaan performers belonging to the Kuthakuthi Hirapara and Khamari Bharigaan troupes. For secondary data, books, articles, and research works available in this respect are taken into consideration. So far the methods are concerned the present study is undertaken adopting descriptive and analytical approaches.

The investigator reviewed available literary writings on Bharigaan as a whole. The literature of Bharigaan is not so vast. Yet mention must be made of the limited but valuable works. Dr.Upendrajit Sarma was awarded Ph.D dgree by Gauhati University for his research work on Comparative Study between KhuliaBhauriya and Bharigaanin the year 2005. Then, Dr. M.Gopal Singha's "Asomor Paribaishya kola: Bharigaan," is a valuable research oriented book on the Bharigaan as a performing art form written in Assamese language. His book deals in detail about the origin and development, subject, features, language, instruments, costumes, beliefs, troupes of performers of Bharigaan. In addition five dramas and two songs of Bharigaan theatre are also enclosed in the mentioned book. Apart from books, writings on Bharigaan are also available in the forms of articles. For example, Dr. Nabin Chandra Sarma discusses Bharigaan at length in his book entitled "Bharatar Uttar Purbanchalar Paribeshya Kala". Then, Dr. Upendrajit Sarma discusses Bharigaan/Bhaugaan theatre tradition of West Assam in his book "Paschim Axomor Lokanatya." Next, Sailen Bharali talks about Bharigaan in short in his article on "Folk

Dramas of Assam" published under the title "Traditional performing Arts of North East India." The same also introduces Bharigaan in brief in the book "Asamiya Loka-Natya-Parampara." Again, "A Critical Study of the Ramayana Tradition of Assam" by Dr. B.K. Deva Goswami also deals with Bharigaan. Lastly, the book under the title "Asomiya Lokonatya: Aitiyya Aru Adhunikata" is a valuable collection of seminar papers with especial reference to Bharigaan.

Bharigaan is a very significant folk theatre of Pati-Rabhas residing in the south Goalpara and Kamrup districts. This has been playing a major role by passing down Rama Tradition to the folk along with some entertainment. It belongs to the Purnanga Natak.According to B.K. Deva Goswami, Bhari gaan" may be a corrupt form of Bhauria, an actor-performer where bhao stands for acting.

Thus the etymology of the term Bhao gaan may be interpreted like bhao, i.e., acting and gan performance,both taking together mean 'an acting performance'. (Goswami 124)

In addition Goswami is of the opinion that Bharigaan bears similarity with Khuliya bhauriya. (Goswami 124) Next Dr. Nabin Chandra Sarma holds the view that the Bhari means weight. Since the masques and other instruments of Bharigaan are too heavy to carry from village to village the troupes of it consider it as Bharigaan (songs of weight). (296-297) Moreover, some are of the opinion that it is called as Bharigaan considering its seriousness of subject matter. Bharigaan is the product of a team work so far the successful staging of the performance is concerned. There are the Oja, Dohari, Palis, Bain and JhaliBojuwa, and Bhaorias in the Bharigaan troupe. The Oja or Mul Gayak Or Geedal is the chief performer of the Bharigaan performance. The Oja of Bharigaan has got similarity with the Sutadhar of Ankia Nat or Bhauna. The Oja is the director, singer and narrator of the whole performance from beginning to the ending. He also introduces all the characters of the drama on the stage to the audience. With a whisk in his hand the Oja maintains coordination among the music, recitation, story and action. The Dohari refers to the Main assistant of the Oja. He is well efficient in songs, verses and dance. Palis are the assistants of the Oja. Normally there are 10 to 15 Palis to assist the Oja. The Palis repeat the songs and verses initiated by the Oja accompanied by dance. Then, there are usually two Bains and two JhaliBajuwa who play the 'Khul' and 'Taal' respectively. Sometimes the number can increase to four persons in each case of the instrument. Bhaoria refers to the actors on the stage successfully portraying different characters according to the demand of the story or play. Such as Sita, Ram, Lakshamana, Ravana, Bibhisan, Kali, Siva, Durga, Hanuman etc. Here, one very noteworthy fact is that no female actor is allowed to perform in Bharigaan even though the character is a female one like Sita or Mandudari. The Mul carries a 'Suwar' (Whick) in his hands while leading the theatre by the performance with gestures and postures.The different instruments used in Bharigaan are -Suwar (whisk), Nupur (jingling anklet), Gada (an iron Mace), Bows and Arrows, Stick, Trishul (trident), Hengdang (Traditional Ahom sword), Khaja Banduk (handmade Rifle) and Swords. In Bharigaan music plays a pivotal role. Here the only musical instruments used are 'Khul' (traditional drum) and 'Taal' (cymbals). At least one pair of each musical instrument is necessary for the performance. The 'taal' is made of bell metal on the other hand khul is, now a day, made of wooden log. Sometimes Flute is also played in some performances of Bharigaan.

As all the dramas of the world have originated from religious beliefs, Bharigaan is not an exception to it. It is a religious folk drama. Here the supernatural power of God is praised. The Bharigaan inspired by Rama-Katha recognizes Rama as incarnation of God Krishna or Narayana.

O he sare bedar sar Ram avatar (Singha 28)

(O incarnated Rama is the essence of the four Vedas.)

Mantri bole Maharaja amara basan
Aboise janiba Raja Ram Narayana (Singha 106)

(The minister says O king listen to my words king Rama is none but Lord Narayana.)

The Pati-Rabha people love to see Rama on stage in Bharigaan as a layman with all limitations of a human being though, he is an incarnation of lord Krishna. This enables lord Rama to enter the heart of folk people being one of them.

Age jhaire Ram Lakhan pase Hanuman
Gala Gali Kari dutir bhai jurila krandan (Singha 136)

(Ram Lakshmana walked ahead followed by Hanuman. Then both brothers started crying embracing each other.)

According to Dr. M Singha in Bharigaan theatre Geet Bandana takes place immediately after khul bandan and before the actual drama starts. Here lord Ramachandra is worshiped for his fine qualities.

The costume of the Bharigaan is an especial element to be discussed. Varied attractive masques are used by different characters of Ramayana. Such as Ravana,Nilakanta, Sugriva,Hanuman, Yamraj, Niljit, Mahadev, Durga etc. Only the Rama, Sita, Lakshaman and Katuwa do not wear a mask. The Pati Rabhas have their distinctive folk beliefs related to the masks. They believe that different spirits reside in the masks. Therefore they are kept separately and worshiped. The masks are usually made of Mango, Coral and 'Satiyana' (Assamese name) tree's wood. Moreover, blue, red, white, yellow are the preferred colours. Here, one very important fact to be mentioned is that the masks do not have holes in the eyes. Because of this the characters wearing masks have to walk and act very carefully like blindfolded. Therefore, the Ravana character wearing huge masks of ten heads takes help of two assistants while performing on the stage. So far dresses of Bhari gaan are concerned; it is found that Ravana is allowed to use royal dress while Rama Sita and Lakshman are considered as common people. Rama is seen in Bharigaan as an exiled man. He and Lakshmana wear attire of deer's skin and grow matted hair like the hermits. Moreover, they are carry bows and arrows.

Shri Rama aal re...Shri Rama Jatha
Dhare re Rama aailre
Sitapati Rama aailRaghupati Rama ailore
Shri Rama aailare Shri Rama Jatha
Dharere Rama aailre
Haste Dhenu Rama aailare. (Singha 183)
Sri Rama comes here...Sri Rama is here with matted hair
Slowly Rama comes
Lord of Sita, Lord of Raghu Bagsha, here comes Sri Ram.
Here comes Sri Ram with matted hair
Slowly Rama comes
Rama comes with bow and arrows in hands.

Although folk drama primarily relies on dialogues, Bharigaan do not consider dialogues to be obligatory. The characters without masks are portrayed with the help of dialogues. Characters with masks on the other hand mainly rely on song oriented presentation on the stage. In addition the roles of females are also performed by the males, for example the role of Sita is played by a male.

Theatres of Bharigaan are traditionally transmitted in a verbal way. Therefore, some variations are seen in the folk dramas. Dr. M. Singha has been successful to record a few of them based on Ramakatha. They are Ravan Badha, Mahi Badha, Patal Kanda and Sakkti khel.

Ravan Badha: The Ravana Badha drama is considered as the most famous theatre amongst the Pati-Rabhas..The story starts after abduction of Sita by Ravana and leads to the much awaited death of Ravan. In course of the progress of the story Rama and Laksman kill Nilajit and Nilkanta. Here Rama also worships Bhagawati Durga to enable him to defeat Ravan in war. The characters of this drama are-Ram, Lakshmana,Dora ketuwa, Mara Ketowa,

Kabiraj, Ravan, Niljit, Nilkanta,Sarathi, Mandudari, Bhibhisan, Hanuman, Sugriva, Maa Durga, Maa Bhagawati etc.

Sakti Khel: Sakti Khel drama's subject matter is serious injury of Laksman in war and his subsequent recovery. Patra, an assistant of Ravana advices, him to kill Lakshmana and says that Rama will die naturally by the unbearable death shock of his beloved brother. So, in war Ravana applies Sakti khel weapon on Lakshmana and nearly kills him. Rama, then calls the Baidya Sachin to rescue his brother. After observing Lakshmana, Sachin advices Rama to bring some magical herbs from Ganda mount. At this Hanuman was called upon to do the job. Subsequently, Hanuman lifted the whole mountain as he could not remember the herb's names. Finally, Lakshman was brought back to life. Some characters of this drama are Rama, Lakshmana, Hanuman, Sachin Baidya, Bharat, Satrughna, Kampali, Seven sisters, Yam Raja, Siva, Sugriva, Jambuvan, Patra etc.

Mahi Badha: The Mahi Ravana theatre mainly deals with the abduction of Rama and Laksmana by Mahit Ravana,brother of Ravana. The Mahit Ravana in disguise of Bibhikhan, takes away Ram and Lakshman to Patal to sacrifice them in front of Goddess Kali. Then, Hanuman, the devotee of lord Rama, enquires the matter with help of Yamraj and Siva and discovers them in Patal puri. Finally, he rescues them by using his intelligence and killes Mahit Rabhana. This theatre brings forth the heroism and devotion of Hanumana. Ravana, at the same time considers the character of Rama simply as a human being in spite of his incarnation on earth.

Ha bhai Lakhan bali kandite lagil
Athaite jadi thakite jadi pawane nandan
Uddhar karate pare bhai duijan. (Singha 168)

(Rama started crying, saying–alas brother Lakshmana if Pawan Nandan would have been here, he would have rescued us.)

Hanuman on the other hand is very much aware of the fact that Rama is none but Lord Krishna.

Hanumane bule gosai kari nibedan
Nakandio prabhu ghane nakar bhabana
Debar devata tumi boikunthar karta
Tumi kena bhoi kara trijagatar dhata (Singha 147)

(Hunuman said-o Lord, I earnestly pray to do not cry or be anxious. You are the God of gods and the ruler of Vaikuntha (the paradise of Vishnu). O the creator of the three universes, why do you fear ?

In Bharigaan after the Vandana song (song of invocation), Oja starts the drama with a song. Immediately after this song two boys with a sage enter the stage and dances for half an hour. These two preteens called as Lakharsuwa are symbolic representation of Rama and Laksmana. On the other hand,the sage is none other than the Vishvamitra, preceptor (Guru) of Rama and Lakshmana. Later in Ravan Badha theatre, the matured Rama is replaced by this preteen Rama for some time during the war when he (Rama) fights with Ravana while sitting on the shoulders of Hanuman. The oja informs this technical matter to the audience very conveniently. Moreover, one very interesting fact is that, in selection of performer for Rama's character, dark skin is preferred. It is because people consider Rama and Krishna as alike. On the other hand, light skin is preferred for Lakshmana's character. In addition, the performers of Rama and Laksmana's character must be expert dancer with proper knowledge of war tactics.

> Folk and popular drama must use a wide variety of techniques to focus the attention of the audience on the performance. Consequently, one encounters clowning, dancing, singing, instrumental music, bombastic speeches, and other highly specialised types of performance as part of the repertoire of effects in countryside drama. (Dorson 354).

Bharigaan also uses different techniques to catch the attention of its audience. For example there is comic character like Ketuwa, assistant of Ravana, makes Bharigaan an amusing folk drama. He entertains the people by his dancing, singing and funny comments. This character is actually not a part of Balmiki Ramalore but creation of Rabha folk minds.

The language of Bharigaan is a mixture of Assamese and Bengali in one hand, Rabha and Assamese on the other hand. In addition, Hindi language is also used. Because of such blending of folk languages, the Bharigaan is so close to Rabha people.

Folk beliefs and customs are very much associated with the Bharigaan. The tribal people believe that the masks possess supernatural power. So they are kept in worship hall or under the observation of the Oja and prayers are offered to them on occasions like Bihu, Shyama Puja and Sangkranti etc. The Pati-Rabhas never keep the masks of Ravana family and the masks of Monkey's family together. They believe that in such a situation, at night, the masks fight and the masks of the defeated party break down by falling on floor. The mask of Kali is kept on the roof of the Oja's house maintaining some rituals so that nobody can touch it. The mask makers also follow some rituals. A particular mask maker cannot produce masks of two opponent group's characters like Hanuman and Nirman etc. During the Kali dance after the sunrise in Ravan Badh drama, some audiences are seen in a fit of madness. People believe that person bearing Libra zodiac sign normally become victim. On such a situation the Oja makes the person comfortable with the help of his whisk.

Bharigaan gives noteworthy examples of material culture of the Pati Rabhas as there are references of folk food items.

Bhat bese brajen bese aru bese pitha
Prabhu jaganathar annna khaite lage Mitha. (Singha 100)

(Rice, curry and pitha/cakes are sold delicious are Lord Jagannath's blessed foods.)

Bharigaan is a distinctive performing art form. It reflects the beliefs, customs and spirit of the tribe in the form of a folk drama. This art form is facing a declining trend in its popularity in a market driven competitive world where entertainment is unlimited and easy to access by just clicking the mouse or button of an electronic gadget. Hence, it is high time to give a new life or form to Bharigaan to survive in the present scenario. We also need to analyse systematically the causes of its decline. Among its various causes we can point out to change of society, profession, economic system, moral values along with mode of entertainments in general. Apart from these, there are some drawbacks in the Bharigaan as a folk theatre itself which needs to be rectified in time to enable it to meet up the question of cultural sustainability. Firstly, the performance of Bharigaan takes a whole night from evening to morning which is a big question to the modern life with shortage of time. Hence, care should be taken of the time factor, enabling everybody to see the drama in spite of the busy schedule. Secondly, the masks of the performing art form are responsible to a large extent for its declining popularity. A character's performance is restricted severely on the stage due to heavy weight and lack of holes on the masks. For example, the Ravana with twelve heads mask has to be controlled by two assistants with the help of ropes from behind during the performance. This act looks very vulgar withdrawing the interest of the audience. Moreover, the weight of the masks makes the performance clumsy and challenging for the new generation to learn. So masks should be prepared in such an innovative way that the above problems do not continue. Thirdly, the dance forms needs to speed up to draw attention of the audience uninterrupted. In addition, such a drama form faces a great threat to survive with its limited audience. Therefore, we need to provide Bharigaan drama a larger audience. Fifthly, the poor financial condition of the performing troupe is causing a threat to the sustainability of the Bharigaan. So, proper financial support should be provided to them to take it as a full time profession.

Conclusion

Bharigaan reflects the life and culture of the Pati-Rabha. It is a splendid fusion of great tradition and small tradition as described by the scholars of folklore. Moreover, this folk drama is not merely an entertaining performing art form but very much reflection of Pati-Rabha people's emotions, philosophy and culture, keeping into consideration the Ramakatha tradition. The Rama, an incarnation of lord Narayana, in spite of being a prince leads a humble life for fourteen years in exile just like any lay person. He has proved himself as best son, king, warrior and devoted husband by facing all sufferings of human life. The same can be observed in case of Sita and Lakshmana also. This fact encourages the folk people to live a righteous life while encountering the bitter sufferings of day to day life. The next important fact is that proper research should be done considering Bharigaan as folk theatre, as it is facing threatening from the world of mass media entertainment. The performers of these theatres should be given a proper platform in the world of entertainment and art by enabling them to take the Barigaan as their profession.

Works Cited

1. Dorson, Richard M,ed. Folklore and Folklife. Chicago: The university of Chicago P., 1972. Print.
2. Iyengar, K.R. Shrinivas,ed. Introduction.Procedings of papers presented at the International Seminar on Variations in Ramayana in Asia: Their Cultural, Social and Anthropological Significance. January 8-10,1981. Asian Variations in Ramayana. 2nd ed. New Delhi : Sahitya Academy, 1983.Print.
3. Goswami, B.K. Deva. A Critical Study of the Ramayana Tradition of Assam. Calcutta: Punthi Pustak, 1994. Print.
4. Grierson,George. Languages of North-Eastern India. 2Vols. India: Gyan Publishing House, 2000. Print.
5. Singha, Dr. M Gopal. Asomar Paribaishyakola: Bharigan. Guwahati: Angik Prakashan, 2015. Print.

Bibliography

1. Bharali,Dr Sailen. Natak Aru Axomiya Natak. Guwahati: Chandra Prakashan, 1990. Print.
2. ---. Asamiya Loka-Natya Parampara. Guwahati: Chandra Prakashan, 2012. Print.
3. Bora, Dr. Mahendra. Sahitya-Upacramanika. Dibrugarh: Dibrugarh, 1985. Print.
4. Dorson, Richard M,ed. Folklore and Folklife. Chicago:The university of Chicago P., 1972.Print.
5. Dutta Dr.Birendra Nath,ed. Traditional Performing Arts Of North –East India. Guwahati: Assam Academy for Cultural Relations,1990.Print.
6. Goswami, B.K. Deva. A Critical Study of the Ramayana Tradition of Assam.Calcutta: Punthi Pustak, 1994. Print.
7. Grierson, George. Languages of North-Eastern India.2Vols.India:Gyan Publishing House, 2000. Print.
8. Hakacham, Dr. Upen Rabha.Rabha Loka-Sanskriti. Guwahati: Pulication Board Assam, 2006. Print.
9. Iyengar, K.R. Shrinivas,ed. Procedings of papers presented at the International Seminar on Variations in Ramayana in Asia: Their Cultural, Social and Anthropological

Significance. January 8-10,1981. Asian Variations in Ramayana.
2nd ed. New Delhi : Sahitya Academy,1983.Print.

10. Rabha, Dr. Malina Devi, ed. Asamar Janajati Aru Sanskrit. Jorhat: Assam Sahitya Sabha, 2011. Print.
11. ---. Rabha Sahityar Buranji. Vol-1. Assam: M.F.L. Publication, 2002. Print.
12. Raghavan, V,ed. Proceedings of papers presented at the International Seminar on The Ramayana Tradition In Asia. December 8-12, 1975.The Ramayana Tradition in Asia. New Delhi: Sahitya Academy,1980.Print
13. Rajbongshi, Dr. Paramananda.ed. Asamar Lokanatya Aru Darangar Khulia Bharia. Darrang:Darrang Zila Sahitya Sabha, 2004. Print.
14. ---.Asomiya Natak: Parampara Aru Paribartan. Guwahati: Chandra Prakashan, 1995. Print.
15. Sarma, Dr. Nabin Chandra. Bharatar Uttar-Purbanchalar Paribeshya Kala. Guwahati: Banalata, 2009. Print.
16. Sarma, Dr. Upendrajit. Paschim Axomor Lokonatya. Guwahati: Rekha Prakashan, 2014.Print.
17. Singha, Dr. M Gopal. Asomar Paribaishyakola: Bharigan. Guwahati: Angik Prakashan, 2015. Print.

प्रदेश

Chapter XII

Relevance of Ram's Philosophy in Contemporary Society

Dr. Sashapra Chakrawarty

The aim of this article is to highlight and capture the vision of Ram and to make it relevant in today's contemporary society. The article addresses how values, morals and principles contained in Ram's story can be practiced in teaching-learning process, for the formation of the whole person and full flowering of the human being and character building. The notion of holistic student development encompasses not only learning academic knowledge and skills, such as problem-solving and analysis, but also other aspects of students as people who are growing and maturing effectively (emotionally) and morally. Thus, the moral, ethical and spiritual development of students must be the fundamental goal of education. The values as given by Rama have to be woven into the curriculum, school environment, and teaching-learning process in a way that these facilitate transmission of values in children in particular and society at broader level.

After seventy years of independence though there have been progress in different fields like economic, scientific, research, technology and educational, but then it is difficult to say whether we are really moving towards creation of happy and worthy society. In recent times, quality education has been defined in more pragmatic terms. It has become synonymous with employability, preparation for the world of work, less and less consideration is given to the subject of education i.e. individual student and his/her full development as a human being. Quality of education should not be considered in fragmented terms but in a more holistic and expanded manner not in terms of number of years of schooling but the quality aspect of the development of the individual. There is no denial that the purpose, the aim, and drive of the educational institutes, must be to equip the students with the most excellent technological proficiency so that students may function with clarity and efficiency in the modern world. But, a far more important purpose than this is to create the right climate and environment so that students may develop fully as total human beings (Krishnamurti 1981: 18). 'Total human being' means not only a human being with inward understanding, with a capacity to explore, to examine his or her inward state and the capacity of going beyond it, but also someone who is good in what he or she does outwardly. The two must go together. That is the real issue in education: to see that when the students leave the school, they are well established in goodness, both outwardly and inwardly (Krishnamurti 2000: 26).

The most important idea governing the ancient system of education was that of perfection, for developing the mind and soul of man. Ancient Indian education aimed at helping the individual to grow in the power and force of certain large universal qualities which in their harmony build a higher type of manhood. The ancient Indian educational system focussed on building a disciplined and values-based culture. Human values such as trust, respect, honesty, dignity, and courtesy are the building blocks of any free, advanced society (Markandan 2005: 92).

Before ancient period Indian Mythology is one of the richest elements of Indian Culture, which enriches it further and makes it a unique one in the world. It has a greatest place in our education system. Through generations, different stories and epic of Indian mythology have been passed from generation to generation either by word of mouth or through carefully stored scriptures. The stories in Indian mythology vary from subtle maxim conveying tales of Panchatantra and Jataka-tales to subtle life paradigm defining stories from the Bhagvad-Gita, Ramayana and Mahabharata. Out of all, the story of Ramayana has a significant place. The popularity of the Rama-story spread throughout not only in India but at world level so widely that, the story is heard or read with pleasure and piety in the palaces as well as in the hovels. The excellence of this unique story enchants the hearts of the rich and poor, of the advanced and under privileged, of the intellectuals and illiterates as well as of the urban and rural people. Fr. C. Blucke rightly says that "the popularity of the Valmiki Ramayana and the voluminous Rama-Literature of many centuries is a monument to the idealism of India, its high esteem of moral values and its belief in the ultimate triumph of good over evil. In the same way, the enthusiastic response of the millions of Indians to the message of Ramacharitamanasa testifies the deep-seated religious belief and spontaneous piety of the soul of India."

Relevance of Rama's philosophy in contemporary society

The story of Rama teaches us the threefold Dharma (code of conduct) pertaining to the individual, the family and the society. Everyone needs to follow the ideals of the Ramayana. The Ramayana speaks of the true identity of the individual, the real significance of the family, and the sanctity of the society.

The Ramayana teaches the importance of human values. Rama stands as a shining example of upholding the moral values in the society. Keeping in mind all the important values, ideals and principles the authors tried to explain some of the important values and morals which are very much required in today's contemporary society.

- **Rama displayed his virtue of self-control:** when he was asked to proceed to the forest for exile on the eve of his coronation, he readily agreed. He maintained his equanimity in the face of adversities unaffected by pain and pleasure, victory and defeat, gain and loss. Today, man aspires for positions of authority though he does not deserve them. But, Rama relinquished exalted position even though he deserved it.
- **Rama always followed his promise:** at any cost. In fact, he went to forest to make his father's promise to Kaikeyi true. Most important are the promises to sages to save their lives from Rakshasas, getting back Sugreeva's kingdom, making Vibhishana the king of Lanka. In the same way a leaders should stand to his promises so as to build relationship with their stakeholders.
- **Excellent friend:** Rama had very touching relations with his friends irrespective of their status. Some of his friends are Nishada - raja Guha, King of Nishaadas (a caste whose profession was hunting the birds), Sugreeva (the Vanar king) and Vibhishana a Rakshasa. In the same way a leaders should stand to his promises so as to build relationship with employees and followers.
- **Great Nobility and Virtue**: Even towards his enemies, Rama showed great nobility and virtue. He always believed in his team and its strength.
- **Embodiments of Love:** Life is like a game of chess; not merely that, it is like a battlefield. Rama is the ocean of compassion. He is love personified. It is possible to understand His divinity only through the path of love. Love is the undercurrent of human life. Man will be able to manifest his innate divinity only when he develops love within.
- **Threefold Dharma (code of conduct):** The story of Rama teaches us the threefold Dharma (code of conduct) pertaining to the individual, the family and the society. You have to make every effort to understand the duties of the individual, the family and the society.

The modern society needs to follow the Dharma that is contained in the epic Ramayana. What is the reason? Today, the son is not paying heed to his father's advice and the parents are not concerned about the future of the son. Devotion to the Guru should be the aim of the students. But, the students are not having regard for their teachers and the teachers are not imparting anything good to them. In such a situation, everyone needs to follow the ideals of the Ramayana

- The Ramayana centres on the principle of **unity in diversity.** All of us live on the same earth. The same sky is above all of us. We breathe the same air and drink the same water. Ignoring this underlying principle of unity man visualizes multiplicity, which is a big mistake. The Ramayana centres on the principle of unity in diversity. Today as man has lost the ability to see unity in diversity, he is immersed in restlessness. What we need today is to see unity in diversity and the divinity behind this unity.
- The other qualities of Ram are
  - He is humble, dignified, a perfect personification of The Ideal Human Being
  - Provide a concrete vision to followers
  - Believe in the ability of subordinates to achieve an aim and inspire them to do so
  - Treat all people equally
  - Stand courageously in the face of great adversity
  - Stand for morality but do not engage in judgmental posturing
  - Consult subordinates on important matters and allow them to give their opinions freely
  - Follow a code of ethics and be ready to sacrifice to follow it

Integrations of Ram's Value system in Teaching Learning System

In the present society moral, religious and spiritual education is being deliberately neglected in our educational system. India is passing through a period of value crisis. Again the National Policy of Education (1986) made the following observation about the value system prevalent in our society. "The erosion of values is now a national phenomenon, so complex and gigantic that a more balanced curriculum, new learning materials and competent teachers, alone can correct this phenomenon."

Today many people read the holy Ramayana, but few understand its essence. They spend their time in acquiring bookish knowledge and superficial knowledge, but fail to have practical knowledge. There are many people who can explain the teachings of Ramayana in a beautiful way, but how many of them obey the command of their fathers in their daily life? Not many! What is the use of reading various texts, if we do not put into practice the message contained in them? Can anyone enjoy the taste of various delicious items such as Mysore Pak, GulabJamoon, Jalebi, etc., by merely repeating their names? No. One can enjoy the taste only when one eats them. Mere textual information is of no use. But, man today is interested only in information, and not transformation. Intellect will blossom only when there is transformation.

The values have to be woven into the curriculum, school environment, and teaching-learning process in a way that these facilitate transmission of values in children. The lesson in any subject, be it Mathematics, Civics, Hindi, Science or English may be designed, deliberated upon, and imparted in such a way that they necessarily invite value related reflection and action in a natural fashion. Values can be imbibed consciously by linking ethics to curricular areas. For example through: Languages- story and dramatization on social evils. Science- values behind scientific research. History- facing historical issues and reacting to them. Social Science, Geography – How different living conditions affect cultures, value systems and behaviours. Physical Education – Competition versus co-operation in sports, sporting/team spirit.

Role of Teacher and Classroom Practices

Teachers conduct the symphony of education. Success of the initiative for values development in students substantially depends on the vision, motivation, skills, attitudes, values and behavior of teachers themselves. It is for this reason that a teacher is compared to a gardener who plants seeds of knowledge and values in students, waters them with care and kindness. It is his/her attitudes, values and relationships that determine the nature of the classroom climate.

One of the important ways of maintaining discipline in classroom is to provide clarity about rules and expectations so that students become conscious about following the rules. Indirect reminders for adhering to the rules can also be put up on the board or by way of posters like "we shall listen to one another, we shall seek permission before speaking, we shall let others learn," etc. the other different ways are

- Using non-verbal ways or signals
- Freedom for Expression
- Constructive Feedback
- Positive Reinforcement
- Accepting Mistakes
- Avoiding Impulsive Judgements and Evaluative Remarks

- Respecting Ideas and Questions
- Increasing Intrinsic Motivation

Role of Co-curricular and Other Activities

- **Silent sitting:** It has been considered an important strategy which helps in the habit of sitting quietly, strengthening the inner being or self, consolidating information received and retaining what is essential. It helps in concentration and assimilation, clear thinking, memory, health, vigor and also helps to be in tune with oneself.
- **Visual experiences:** Learning through visual experiences such as symbols, drawings, poster, charts, cartoons, graphs, photographs and pictures, and auditory and kinesthetic experiences compared to verbal mode, are less abstract and more powerful for communication of attitudes and values and forming imagery at the early primary years of schooling.
- **Prayer:** The habits of prayer must be deeply inculcated in the students. It develops faith, devotion and self-confidence. It is a safe outlet for pent-up feelings and frustrations. It also improves memory and concentration and infuses strength and courage and confers mental peace.
- **Stories:** Stories have always been considered to be the best way to get across an important value based message.
- **Religious Celebration:** The corporate life of school can be made an important medium of giving religious, especially moral education. Teachers and students get a golden opportunity of mutual relationship, and listing and learning moral values.
- **Sports and Playground:** The qualities of cooperation, goodwill and equality can very be developed through sports activities. The value of punctuality and equality emerges in the playground.
- **Cultural Programmes:** It undoubtedly develops good and refined tastes and tells us about our culture. National, historical, social and religious festivals can be celebrated. Folk-song, dramas, folk dance, comedy, folk stories can be performed in such cultural programmes.
- **Role playing:** Role play is a type of imaginative play, where children assume roles outside their real world place. Role play allows children to construct proximities between themselves and others in their lives.
- **Group Singing:** Music speaks the language of the heart. Group singing transcends artificial barriers of gender, ethnicity, race, and socio-economic distinctions and inspires a spirit of unified community

and co-operation. Songs internalize the universal message of the values and promote feelings of joy, harmony and confidence within the group and within each child.

- **Group Activities:** It provides opportunities for learning of many values concurrently. Development of fundamental values of love, tolerance, cooperation, peaceful co-existence and respect for others is important.

Conclusion

The purpose of education and the concern for quality education should not only be in terms of employability and economic progress but, also individual's holistic development as a human being, so that he/she lives creatively and happily, and also contributes to the welfare of the society. Concern for peace and values need to be viewed as core component of quality and not merely as value premises.

References

1. Reference: Markandan, N. (2001), 'The Value and Purpose of Education', in Samir Banerjee and Sanjeev Ghotge, eds, Contributions Towards An Agenda For India, pp. 91–93 (Shimla: Indian Institute of Advanced Study).
2. Krishnamurti, J. (2000), Life Ahead (Chennai: Krishnamurti Foundation).
3. http://cbseportal.com/exam/e-books/download-free-ncert-e-book-education-for-values-in-school-a-framework\.
4. http://cbseacademic.in/web_material/ValueEdu/Value%20Education%20Kits.pdf

Chapter XIII

Assessment of Rama's story and Character in Sankardeva's 'Ramvijay-nat' and its Relevance at Present Time

Dr. Subhra Sabhapandit

MahapurushShrimantaSankardeva has composed six one act plays (ankiyanats) extracting subjectmatters from the Bhagavatpurana, Harivamsa and the Ramayana. Sankardeva is the pioneer of the Bhakti movement in Assam. The idea of Bhakti movement is that all living beings are the parts of Lord Vishnu and hence there is no division among them. Bhaktivada has taken an idea of Advaita philosophy according to which, there is no existence of duel entities. That is to say there is only one supreme power or self (Lord Vishnu of Bhaktivada). 'Ek Saran Nam Dharma' of Sankardeva believes in the worship of Lord Vishnu. Shrimanta Sankardeva chooses the aesthetic form to spread the Bhakti movement, because art can always appeal the common people. Through his ankiyanats and borgeets, Sankardeva has brought a new renaissance of Bhakti. In his dramas all people can participate, there is total participation of whole community. This is a great contribution of Sankardeva to social integration.

'Ramvijay' is the last one act play written by Sankardeva in the 1568 A.D. This play is written by Sankardeva in Kochbihar at the request of prince Cilarai. The plot of this play is extracted from the Adikanda of the Ramayana. The plot deals with the subject-matter from the 19th to the 77th cantos of the Adikanda of the Ramayana. The story includes how sage Visvamitra takes with him Rama and Laksmana to destroy the demons Maric and Subahu, who obstructed the hermits in their performance of sacrifices; after destruction of the demons, arrival of Visvamitra in Mithila with Rama and Laksmana; Rama's marriage with Sita after breaking the bow of Lord Siva; their return journey to Ayodhya where Rama is confronted with Parasurama and the defeat of Parasurama in the hands of Lord Rama.Sankardeva has reformed the original story with his descriptive and imaginative powers. His poetic genius is revealed in this play. In the Ramayana Visvamitra seeks Dasaratha's permission to take only Rama (Valmiki 1/19/8) with him for ten days (Valmiki 1/19/14) to kill the demons who have obstructed the sacrifice,though Laksmana also goes with Rama. But in the play the sage asks both Rama and Laksmana and there is no mention of any time. In the origin Dasaratha shows his unwillingness to send Rama with Visvamitra. Then sage Vasistha tries to convince Dasaratha. He says that Visvamitra is the embodiment of dharma. No other person in the world has such intellect and prowess like him. In these statements Visvamitra's greatness is revealed in the Ramayana (Valmiki 1/21/10-12). In the play Ramvijay the sage Vasistha does not even appear. So here Visvamitra's greatness is also not revealed properly. Moreover, as Dasaratha suddenly changes his mind and becomes ready to send Rama with the sage, so this aspect of his fickle-mindedness decreases the seriousness of the character. In the origin Dasaratha shows many reasons for not sending Rama and also requests Visvamitra to allow him to go with Rama- "caturangasamayuktammayasaha ca tat naya|" (Valmiki 1/20/1-14). But in the play Dasaratha himself wants to go instead of Rama and Laksmana- "rama-laksmana se balaka| … hamakaniya java|" (Sankardeva 43).

In the origin Visvamitra discusses many subjects with Rama and Laksmana during their journey. But Sankardeva has omitted many of these. Bestowing of two vidyas, viz., bala and atibala by Visvamitra to Rama in the bank of river sarayu in the 22nd canto, description of the hermitage ananga by Visvamitra in the 23rd canto, description of the origin of Malada and Karusa states and the description of Tadaka in the 24th canto, bestowing of various weapons by Visvamitra to Rama in the 27th canto, description of siddhasrama by Visvamitra in the 29th canto¬- these all are omitted by Sankardeva for dramatic purpose. Because of this the unity of action is perfectly maintained. In the origin the hermits have welcomed and pay homage to Visvamitra, Rama and Laksmana at their arrival in the siddhasrama (Valmiki 29th canto). Sankardeva has also omitted this scene to reduce complicacy in the plot, but due to this the glimpse of hermitage culture is disappeared. Description of sagara-race and the long description of Visvamitra's attainment of brahmanya are also omitted regarding these unnecessary for the dramatic effect. In the origin to Visvamitra, Rama and Laksmana, Janaka describes how he achieves Sita and the bow of Lord Shiva (Valmiki 66th canto). These descriptions are also omitted in the Ramvijaynat. The presence of these descriptions may make the play more striking.

According to Valmiki's Ramayana, Visvamitra goes to Mithila with Rama and Laksmana to attend the sacrifice of Janaka. But in the play they goes to the svayambara of Sita- "ajujanakisitakasvayambaramilice|... sohibararamanigharanijabahui|...calaabilambajanakakathama|| sriramachand ratoharisvayambarasuniyeavala|" (Sankardeva 45,47, 50). Sankardeva describes the kings' sensual condition at the glance of Sita- "rajasabakakamabanepidala| madanemanamarddaya| priyehamaka haste parakha|" (Sankardeva 53, 54). He also describes the kings' proceed with ego to break the bow of Lord Shiva and their failure- "paramaarambarekacigiyapahilehidhanukadharala| dasanakamur igunaditecitahuyaparala|" (Sankardeva 55). These descriptions are not found in the Ramayana. Imagination of the kings'sensual condition is low of taste. Moreover, the kings' proceed to break the bow with ego is very much dramatic. Again according to the play Sita believes in the past birth- "se jatismarakany apurbbajanamakakatha cite parala|" (Sankardeva 38, 39). She remembers the boon she has got to have Lord Vishnu as her husband-"hamupurabajanamaisv aranarayanakasvamiicchakayala| arajanamesriramarupetohokabibahakaraba|" (Sankardeva 39). So she feels love for Rama from the very beginning.Sita calls Rama as svami- "ha ramasvami...|" (Sankardeva 39) and becomes overwhelmed when he proceeds to break the bow of Lord Shiva- "bajradhikakathinama hesakadhanu, ihatagunaditesvamijanonahiparaya|" (Sankardeva 56). When Sita puts the garland on the neck of Rama-"svamikamathe mala paridhai|" (Sankardeva 56) then the kings become aggressive "tahepekhirajasabasokakop emohitahuyadhanubanadhariyeramakaparamadarpa kaya garaje|" (Sankardeva 57), Sita becomes overwhelmed-"rajasabakaparamaandolarolasuniyerajanandi nibhayeparamaakulabheli|" (Sankardeva 57) and Rama hugs her- "priyakapara masantapanirekhiramachandrabahumelipriyakadharikahuasvasa kaya bolala|" (Sankardeva 58). These descriptions are not found in the Ramayana. Through these descriptions, Sankardeva's dramatic tricks are revealed. These descriptions also reveal the psychological analysis of the character of Sita. In the origin the announcement from the sky- "tadanantareakasabanisunala: ahekanya, toh oohijanamesvamikabhetanapavaba| arajanameshriramarupetohokabibahakara ba|" (Sankardeva 39) is not found and Sita does not put the garland on the neck of Rama- "dhanuta je gunaditeparayatahekamathekusumamaladiyesitasv amibaraba|" (Sankardeva 54). In the Ramayana Janaka invites Dasaratha and they accomplish the marriage of Rama and Sita. According to the Ramayana, sage Vasistha has performed the homa at the marriage of Rama and Sita- "agnimadhayavedyamtuvidhimantrapuraskritam| juhabagnaumahatejavasi sthomunipungavah||" (Valmiki1/73/24). But in the play the character of Vasistha does not even appear. In the play Visvamitra performs the homa- "visvamitrakusandikariyehomaarambhala|" (Sankardeva 58). At that time Visvamitra is described as affected by sexual feelings which is very low of taste- "sitakabhubanarupanirekhi rishi kame aturabhelaha|" (Sankardeva 59). Again according to the Ramayana, Janaka gives his younger daughterUrmila to Laksmana (Valmiki 7/71/12) and his brother's daughters to Bharata and Satrughna (Valmiki 73rd canto). Omitting the descriptions of these marriages in the play Sankardeva tactfully stays away from any complicacy.

The cause of Parasurama's conflict with Rama shown by Sankardeva is different from that shown by Valmiki. According to Valmiki, Parasurama describes to Rama the details of the bows of Lord Vishnu and Lord Siva. As Rama breaks the bow of Lord Shiva so Parasurama ask him to put arrow in the bow of Lord Vishnu. If he can do that then Parasurama will fight with him (Valmiki 1/75/10-28). But in the Ramvijaynat, Parasurama calls Rama for fight bytaking the axe in his shoulder- "ajutoh kaskandharudhirenikakarabo|" (Sankardeva 61). Sita's worry for Rama- "svamikaalingidhariyejaicebilapakaya la..|" (Sankardeva 62), Rama's consolation-"sapremabanibulias-vasakayala|" (Sankardeva 62), Visvamitra's interference- "hamaraparamasisyaramachandraa-hakabadhyodyamatuhubheli|" (Sankardeva 63), his fight with Parasurama-"aye jatasakatithikaajuhamakayuddhadehu|" (Sankardeva 63)-these descriptions are not present in the Ramayana Sita's worry and Rama's consolation reveal Sankardeva's excellent imaginative power. These descriptions are very much fit for the dramatic effect.

Sankardeva has omitted many characters of the original story and reforms it to make fit for the one act play. On the other hand he has introduced few new characters. Introduction of Sita's friends- "ha hasakhikanakavati...|" (Sankardeva 49) reveals Sankardeva's high imaginativecapacity. Sankardeva also introduces the descriptions of the beauties of Rama- "dasaratharajakuma rakotikandarpadarpadalana..| badanainduparakasa| arunaadharamandahasa|" (Sankardeva 50, 51) and Sita- "kanaka putalitulatanuanupama||" (Sankardeva 46). In this respect there may be the influence of Madhav Kandali's Ramayana (sarmadaloi 18).

In one act play there is very limited scope for the development of the characters. The Ramvijay is the one act play with a limited sphere. Moreover, it is written in lyrical style. So Sankardeva has very little scope for development of all the characters. Inspite of this the main characters of the Ramvijaynat are well developed by Sankardeva with his poetic genius.

In the Ramvijaynat Sankardeva's poetic genius is revealed in the manifestation of rasa (sentiment) also. Almost all the sentiments are suggested in this play. Through the activities of Sita and of the kings coming for the svayambara of Sita, the erotic sentiment is suggested- "bhelipulakatanucetanaakula kamala nayanajhurebari|| sakhikanakavatimadanamantharasitakadharikahuanchor eangamuchiprabodhabolaya|" (Sankardeva 52), "raja nandinikanavayauvana rupalavanyanirekhirajasabakakamabanepidala|" (Sankardeva 53). The heroic sentiment is suggested by the speech of Rama to Parasurama- "raharahaajutuh ujamapuradekhaba| shriramakadhanutankareparasuramakahridayabidarala|" (Sankardeva 65). By the speech of Parasuramara udra-rasa is suggested –"ham uekabinsatibarabhumibhramiyesabaksatriyaramundamaralo| ajutohakaskandh arudhirenikakarabo|" (Sankardeva 61). The hasya-rasa is suggested through the performance of sacrifice by Visvamitra- "hatakasruvasrucakhahiparala| sarirakampimuruciparala|" (Sankardeva 59). In the battle between Visvamitra and Parasurama the vibhatsa-rasa is suggested- "parasuram amahakopedandadharala| visvamitradandadharidhavala|" (Sankardeva 63). Santa-rasa is suggested by the speech of Dasaratha to Visvamitra in Ayodhya- "hamaraputraramalaksmana se balaka| tahekaraksasakadite cava| ohikonabyavahara| ... yajnaraksanimittehamakaniya java|" (Sankardeva 43) and also by the speech of Visvamitra to Rama after the killing of the demons- "tuhuhamaraparamaupakari| tohakagunasujayenahipari| sampratipratyupakar atohokakakaraba|" (Sankardeva 45). Though many rasas are suggested in the play yet sringara and vira are the predominant ones. The sentiment of karuna is also predominantly suggested in this play. Through the worry and lamentation of Sita- "ahesakhisabaparamaabhaginikakipucaha| ...ohibulitesitakaparamasa ntapaupajala|" (Sankardeva 39) and Dasaratha- "raja rishikaaicanabacanasun iyedurantacintayepidala| murcchitahuyaparala|" (Sankardeva 42) the karuna-rasa is successfully suggested. But the important matter to be noticed is that over all these rasas the bhakti-rasa is suggested throughout the whole play.

The ankiyanats of Sankardeva are developed on the basis of Sanskrit dramas and Assamese ojapali-dance, puppet-dance etc. The Ramvijaynat is started with two nandi-verses- "yannamakhilalokasokasamanamyannamaprem aspadam...sadasadaram|| 1 ||""yenabhajidhanuhsivasyasahasasitasamasvasi ta...bhagavanshriramachandrasciram|| 2 ||" (Sankardeva 33). In the first verse Rama is eulogised as the supreme power. In the second verse the subject-matter of the play is indicated. All the five sandhis of Sanskrit drama are present in the Ramvijaynat. Arrival of Visvamitra at the court of Dasaratha and taking with him Rama and Laksmana to the hermitage to protect sacrifice –this part of the story can be considered as mukha-sandhi. Arrival of Rama at the court of Janaka is pratimukha-sandhi. Breaking of the bow of Lord Shiva and gaining Sita is garbha-sandhi. Incidents with the kings at the svayambara of Sita is vimarsa-sandhi. Marriage of Rama with Sita is nirvahana-sandhi.

The language of the dialogues, sutras and geets of the ankiyanats is brajavali. The language of the slokas (verses) is Sanskrit. Only in few payaras the ancient

Assamese language is used. Though in one act plays there is no division of scenes, yet in Sankardeva's ankiyanats we can notice many divisions of scenes. In the Ramvijaynat also this characteristic is present. There are 37 slokas (excluding nandi-sloka), 4 bhatimas, 1 payar and 18 geetas (excluding the pravesa-geeta) in the Ramvijaynat. This play has fulfilled almost all the rules of Sanskrit dramaturgy. Other ankiyanats of Sankardeva have not fulfilled all the rules.

Rama is considered as the epithet of Lord Vishnu. He is a dhirodattatype of hero in Sanskrit literature.Sankardeva also depicts him as this type of hero. He is very handsome. His beauty is superior to that of the God of Love- "kotikandarpadarpadalana.. |" (Sankardeva 50). He comes to this world to remove its stress- "je jagatakaparamaisvara Narayana bhumikabharahar ananimittadasarathagriheavatarala |" (Sankardeva 36). Prowess is the main characteristic feature of Rama. Killing of the demons, protecting the sacrifice of the sages, defeat of his competitors in the svayambara of Sita and the defeat of Parasurama- these all are proving the prowess of Rama. He is polite and obedient to his preceptor, father and other elders. He immediately accepts the order of his preceptor sage Visvamitra. He does not want to show off his prowess. Therefore, when Visvamitra instructs him to break the bow of Lord Shiva, he first bows down to the sage and indicates his incapability- "rishikapranama kaya bola ahemuniraja! hamubalakaohidhan ubajradhikakathina | ihatagunaditehamarasamarthyakaicana hoi | tathapito haraajnapaliyatnakaraba |" (Sankardeva 55). By consoling Sita when she is scared at his confrontation with Parasurama, Rama proves care for his wife- "sapremabanibuliasvasakayala |" (Sankardeva 62). He is also a loving brother- "aye bhaya! Tuhubalakaraharaha | ohidustadvijakahamodandakara bo | tahusukheyuddhadekhaha |" (Sankardeva 64). All the good qualities are revealed in the character of Rama. He is an ideal character for all Indians. As an epithet of Lord Vishnu, Rama is worshiped by all Hindus. In the Ramvijaynat, Sankardeva has effectively presented the character of Rama. Rama's prowess and other qualities can definitely influence the minds of people. Destruction of demons indicates the destruction of evilpower in the society which is very relevant at the present time. The demons have obstructed in the performance of sacrifices. Similarly at present time, many negative powers obstruct in the wellbeing of the society. The evil powers of the society can be removed by taking inspiration from the character of Rama which is very pleasingly presented by Sankardeva in the Ramvijaynat. Moreover, defeat of Parasurama in the hands of Rama suggests the defeat of pride and ego in front of honesty and politeness. These aspects of Rama's character are also beautifully revealed in the Ramvijaynat which can influence people of all classes of the society. Rama is not only a powerful human being, but he is uplifted to the position of parambrahma, i.e., the supreme power- "he prabhoshrirama! tohoparamaisvara|" (Sankardeva 65). So his story and character have great impacts in the minds of all people from the time of the Ramayana. By composing Ramvijaynat Sankardeva also has contributed in this respect. All people cannot understand the Sanskrit language. So they cannot understand Valmiki's Ramayana. The Ramvijaynat is written in the brajavali language which is understood by almost all Assamese people. So the story and character of Rama depicted in this one act play can influence people of all classes of the Assamese society. In the present society youths are devoid of courage, they indulge in inactivity. They can take inspiration from Rama's courage, prowess, valour and activeness. Corruption and other evil and negative things in the society can be removed by taking inspiration from Rama's killing of demons. Sacrifices are performed for the wellbeing of the society. The demons have obstructed in the sacrifices and thus have obstructed in the wellbeing of the society. At present time also some people are doing great for the society. But some negative people are obstructing them. These people can be handled with, by being inspired by the character of Rama. Rama and Laksmana's love bears a great message of brotherhood for the society. Rama's respect for Visvamitra is also influencing. Now a days students have no respect for their teachers. Rama's respect for his teacher may change their thinking. Ego, anger etc. are common characteristics of the people of present society. These emotions are destructing, but people cannot make themselves free from these emotions. Parasurama is an embodiment of anger and ego. His anger and ego are defeated by Rama's calmness, humbleness and politeness. Visvanatha, in his Sahityadarpana, says that poetry (kavya) teaches people to act like Rama, but not like Ravana and other negative characters- "rama divatpravartitavyamnaravanadivat...|" (Visvanatha 3). Poetry thus teaches people what to do and what not to do- "krityakrityapravrittinivrittyupades advarenasupratitaiva|" (Visvanatha 3). Ramvijay is a poetry (drisya-kavya) and it deals itself with the story of Rama. So this play surely teaches people to act like Rama and thus definitely have relevance in the positive change and development of the present society.

Bibliography

1. Bora,Mohim (ed.),"Sankardevar Nat." Publication Board Assam, 1989.
2. Mahanta, Pradipjyoti (ed.), "ShrimantaSankardevaSamajAruSanskriti." Puberun Prakash, Guwahati, 2000.

3. Sankardeva. "Ramvijaynat" ed. by Dr.HarinathSarmadaloi. Chandra Prakash, Guwahati, 1992. 2nd print.
4. Sarma, Satyendranath. "AsamiyaSahityarSamiksatmakItivritta." Saumar Printing and Publishing Company, Guwahati, 1981.
5. Valmiki. "Ramayana" ed. by Robert P. Goldman. MotilalBanarsidass Publishers Private Limited, Delhi, 2007. 1st edition.
6. Visvanatha. "Sahityadarpana" ed. by Sheshraja Sharma Regmi. Krishnadas Academy, Varanasi, 2002. 10th print.

Chapter XIV

Reflection of Assamese Society in the Ramayana of Madhava Kandali

Tina Sarma

Ramayana, the Adikavya of Hindu, is translated into so many languages of India. Among the translations of North-East India, Madhava Kandali's Ramayana is ancient[1]. Therefore, his name and place in Assamese literature are always remarkable. Madhava Kandali is the great Assamese poet of India belonging to the fourteenth century A.D. He is patronised by the Kachari King Mahamanikya to compose this work. He is renowned as Kaviraja. Another work is also attributed to him, the 'Devajit.' But, he is famous for his Ramayana. His Ramayana is considered as the earliest extant work on Assamese literature. Kandali's Ramayana is known as 'Saptakanda Ramayana.' Like the Ramayana of Valmiki, it also includes seven kandas as the name implies. But the story of five kandas is circulated among the people. Some scholars opine that the Adikanda and the Uttarakanda are not found. Therefore, it is found that Madhavdev and Sankardev both compose these two kandas respectively after few years.

Though Kandali's Ramayana is directly a translation of the origin book of Valmiki, the Adikavi, but he reflects the then assamese society of fourteenth century completely. The aim of his translation is to explain the story of the Ramayana in an easy way among the people of Assam, in short. Somewhere, he directly translates the origin text and also somewhere he gives only the inner meaning according to his feelings. In many places of his work, Kandali represents a description of mingling the smell of land and water of Assam without any hamper from original text. Like the reflection of life and culture of India is found in the Ramayana of Adikavi, Kandali also draws a picture of the life of Assamese people in his work. To give a taste of Assamese people, he presents some stories of the day to day life of people of Assam. Therefore, in the work of Kandali, all the sides related to the Assamese society of fourteenth century are reflected as well as the story of Rama. So, the aim of this paper is to show the reflection of Assamese society in the Ramayana of Madhava Kandali.

Reflection of Assamese Society in the Ramayana of Madhav Kandali

The Assamese society, which is drawn by Kaviraja Kandali in his Ramayana, is a farmer living society. Agriculture was the main profession of the then people of Assam. Among agriculture, rice-land is the main. Kandali describes the foods made from rice in his work. Besides these, various crafts and craftsmen related to agriculture are also mentioned in the Ramayana. Kandali describes it in connection with the description of returning of Rama to Ayodhya by Bharata with his subjects[2]. From this description, it is found that besides the four castes, there are also other professional castes in that time like nata, bhata, baniya etc.

The place of women in the society of that time is also depicted in the Ramayana of Madhava Kandali. Freedom of women is not considered in the society of Assam or India from the days of yore. So, woman cannot do anything alone. In this connection, the following verse can be cited from the conversation of Sita and Hanuman from the Ramayana –

Bulibi ravana sito anileka hari
Strijati paradhina nohe svatantari[3]

Though any indication relating to the practise of music and dance is not found to be seen in the time of composing the Ramayana of Madhava Kandali, but it can be assumed from the mentioning of the castes like nata, bhata etc. that dance and music were prevalent at that time also. And the use of various instruments, which are indispensable for performing dance and music, is also mentioned in the work of Kandali. For example, the occasion of coronation is resounded by playing various types of instruments in the time of the coronation of Sugriva[4]. But, Kandali mentions the instruments of Assamese society like dhak, dhol, ramtal, kartal, shankha, mridanga, flute, tokari, dagar, dotara, dundubhi, bina, jijiri, shinga etc. In this connection, it can be mentioned two verses like –

Shankhapata harisara madalara jaka
Nandini ninada badya bave bira Dhaka

Again,

Ghantara shavade hasti cale saharise
Age pase calante turangasava hese

In Assamese society, everybody gives their salute to father, mother or elder at the time of departure for a new journey to do an auspicious work. Kaviraja also displays this rule at the pre-moment of the journey of Hanuman to Lanka[5]. When found an opportunity, Kandali makes his work delicious for the readers by implying the local style. In the descriptions of the houses, he presents a picture of the houses, which are seen in the style of Assam.

In the writings of Kaviraja Madhava Kandali, it is seen that the art of painting has also developed at that time in Assam. Various descriptions of the pictures seen in the walls of the house of Ramachandra indicate that. This expert writer thus proofs the art of painting of Assam.

Again, in the descriptions of food and its constituents, sports and games, ornaments, clothes etc. Kandali gives evidences of the Assamese culture. Regarding the food, Kandali mentions rice, fish, milk, green vegetables, fruits etc. in the list. Again, he says about eating of frumenty, where the rice is boiled in milk and seasoned with sugar. He displays that Dasaratha eats rice[6]. Ramachandra, Lakshman and Sita eat the meat of deer in the forest[7]. Kandali mentions butter and honey also in his work. A refreshing draught consisting of curd, butter, honey, milk and sugar offered to a god i.e. the 'Madhuparka', is also mentioned somewhere.

Though Kandali does not mention directly about the clothes of Assamese people, but the use of the clothes for covering women, divine cloth, turban, armour cloths for battle etc. are seen in the work of Kandali. He tries to show the folk culture of Assam through clothes. The use of white clothes is also found for many occasions[8]. He indicates about the wearing of clothes of God by Ramachandra and silk saree by Sita[9].

Regarding the ornaments, Kaviraja Kandali mentions various types. Among them, Kundal-a kind of ear ornament, Satsari-a necklace of seven strings, ring, Nupur-a jingling anklet, Galpata-a kind of necklace, bangles are found to be used in that time[10]. Besides these, the people of that time of Assam uses fragrant wood, sandal-wood, kajal, red lead, turmeric etc. for make-up. Kandali delineates it at the going of Ramachandra to the house of Kaikeyi[11].

From the time of yore, sports and games take a prominent place among people. In Assam also, various games are played traditionally. The Ramayana of Madhava Kandali, where all the Assamese folk culture has been depicted, also includes the games of Assam. As for example, Kandali describes about the games like ghila, bhanta, the act of striking each other with hand, wrestling, dice used play, gambling play. These are played by the demons at the time of entering Hanuman entering into Lanka.

Nature of Assam also plays a vital role in the work of Kandali. In the descriptions of trees, creepers, fruits etc. he displays the gardens found in the villages of Assam. Sweet fruits are the favourite food for the inhabitants of Lanka. Again, in the descriptions of Chitrakuta and Ashokavana of the Ramayana, Kandali shows his expertise by including the fruits, trees, flowers etc. from the villages of Assam, which are not found to be seen in the original work of Valmiki[12].

Apart from fruits etc., Madhava Kandali also describes the animals and birds, which are usually found in the forests of Assam only, in his work. Among them, the animals like lion, goat, monkey, snake, horse, tiger, bear etc. and the birds like cuckoo, honey-sucker, duck, ordinary goose etc. are found.

The description of state administration of Assam also could not escape the arena of Kandali's writing. He mentions the administrative policy of Assam in connection with the discussion of coronation of Ramachandra by Dasaratha, protection of Lanka by Ravana etc. It can be assumed from the use of the words like sandikoi and paik, that, was prevalent during the Ahom rule in Assam.

Conclusion

From the above discussion on the reflection of Assamese society in the Ramayana of Madhava Kandali, we can conceive the idea that though the work is a translation but it seems as an original work of Kandali by his own power of writing. In his writing, the ultimate picture of Assamese society and folk-culture is reflected. Almost all the aspects of the society of fourteenth century A.D. of Assam are illuminated beautifully in this composition of Madhava Kandali.

Bibliography

A. Original Works:

1. Madhava kandali Saptakandaramayana, pub. by Munshiram Manoharlal Publishers Private. Limited, New Delhi, 2000
2. Valmikiramayanam, edt. by Sivaramasarma vasistha, pub. by Chaukhamba Vidya Bhavan, Baranasi.
3. Srimadbhagavatgeeta, edt. by Khatara Satra, 2011

B. Modern Works:

1. Bora Saikiya, Indira; Ramayani Sahityar Adhyayan, Kiran Prakashan, Dhemaji, Assam, 2005
2. Neog, Dimbeswar; Asamiya Sahityar buranji, Shuwani Prakash, Guwahati
3. Neog, Maheswar; Asamiya Sahityar Ruprekha, Chandra Prakash, Guwahati, 2013
4. Sarma, Satyendranath; Asamiya Sahityar Samikshatmak Itibritta, Pratima Devi, Guwahati, 2004
5. Sarmadaloi, Dr. Harinath; Asamiya Sahityar Purna Itihas, Saraswati Press, Nalbari, 2010

References

1. Sarma, Dr. Satyendra Nath, Assamiya Sahityar Samikshatmak itibritta, pg 76, fifth edition, 1991
2. Khatri baisyagana kayastha sajjana nata bhata teli tanti /
   Thathari sonari kasara sekhari bharatara lage yanti //
   Baniya camara kamara sutara dhoba aru kumbhakara /
   Isava pramukhe calila yateka adi anta nahi tara//ayodhyakanda, 31.3
3. Sundarakanda, 14.130
4. Kiskindhakanda, 17. 9-10
5. Rama lakshmanaka sugriva birata kariya sewa satkara /
   Bayu ye bapaka anjana mavaka pranamila satabara // sundarakanda, 6.1
6. Aji thaki anugraha kariyo amata /
   Pariccheda ake thane bhunjo ami bhata //
   Raghave bolanta bapa shuniyo apane /
   Aji duyo bhata khaibo kali khaibo kone // lankakanda
7. Kato dura goiya bara brikshamula paila /
   Harinake maria randhia toite khaila // ibid
8. Katha shuni kaushalyayo shukla bastra dhari /
   Achanta devar ghare kritanjali kari // ibid
9. Devanga basana tejilanta tetikshane /
   Pindhila bakali bastra shrirama lakshmane //
10. Pindhileka harise batrish alankar/
    Mukuta kundale gribe satsari har//
    Balaya kankana kanchi nupurara saja/
    Hansi keli kare yena sarobara maje// ayodhyakanda, 2284
11. Sarirata pindhileka agaru candana /
    Koikeyira grihe lagi karila gamana //
12. Sarala piyala khara nikhara kharjjura/
    Shala tala tamala gamari bijapura //
    Ashvattha kapittha bata naranga badara/
    Tenteli kantaki ama jama nagesvara //
    Khajuri haritha amalakhi jahaphala/
    Chatiyale gua narikela ye shriphala //
    Salanga mahari aru kamala tengara /
    Kardoi pichumardaka ye solonga amara //
    Kadambagulala parijataka ashesa /
    Seuti malati guti-maliye bishesa // lankakanda

Chapter XV

A Comparative Study of the Character of 'Rāma' in Mādhab Kandali's Rāmāyana and Subhas Bhattacharya's Bengali Translated Rāmāyana named Vālmiki-Rāmāyana

Dr. Dulal Chandra Das

Rāmāyana is the most popular and ancient epics of the world. It was was written by Adi Kabi Vālmiki. According to traditional belief Rāmāyana written by Vālmiki before the birth of Rāma. Vāmiki describes here about the character of Rāma, the son of Dasratha at Ayodhyā. They were known as empire of Iskāku. Vāmiki's Rāmāyana is the main root of the Indian literature. In this reference we mention the opinion of Indirā Goswami,

> The Rāmāyana is a magnificent tree whose shade and roots have spread far and wide. Its shade has provided happiness and solace to souls. Wherever its root has reached, a fruit laden and joy-giving tree has cropped up. Its roots have crossed the island of Bali and Mauritius. It has transmitted its fragrance to Java, Fiji, Trinidad, Surinam, Malaysia, Thailand and Burma. (Indira Goswami: Rāmāyana from Ganga to Brahmaputra, page-09)

North East is one of the most holy places of Hinduism. The study of Vālmiki's Rāmāyana is going on from the very early age in Assam. Mādhab Kandali is one of the earlier popular writers in Rāmāyani Sāhitya, all over India. He translated Vālmiki's Rāmāyana in 14th -15th century. Before Mādhab Kandali no one could translate Vālmiki's Rāmāyana in vernacular language. He is the first translator of Vālmiki's Rāmāyana in India in vernacular language. He completely translated Vālmiki's 'Sapta Kānda' Rāmāyana but, two kandas have not yet been discovered. Mādhab Kandali's principle of translation is-

> Vālmiki rachilā shāstra gadya padya chande;Tāhak bichār āmi kariyā prabandhe.

Aponār budhi artha jimate bujilo;sangsep kariyā tāk pada bichārilo.
Samasta rasaka kone janibāk pāre; pakhisab uray jen pakhā anusāre.
Kobisab nibondhoy loka bybahare;koto nija koto lambha katha anusare.
(Mādhab Kandali: Ramayana,)

(Valmiki wrote in a lyrical prose style. Kandali translated the same to Assamese based on his understanding of Valmiki's lyrical prose. No one can grasp in totality the works of others. Birds can fly according to their wings. In this way the poet translated the Rāmāyana of Valmiki in Assamese for the common people.)

Mādhab Kandali with this principle translated the Rāmāyana of Valmiki to old Assamese language variation. After Kandali's Rāmāyana Tulsi Das in north India, Kritibas in Banga translated Valmiki's Rāmāyana to Hindi and Bangla. Therefore Mādhab Kandali's Rāmāyana is the oldest translated form of Valmiki's Rāmāyana in India. Madhav Kandali has differently described the character of Rāma from other Indian vernacular writers. But he tries to write remaining loyal to the origin. Mainly, he described all the traits of Rāma's character in Valmiki's Rāmāyana in his translation. The Assamese people believe that Rāma is the Eighth avatar of Bishnu. A great impact of Valmiki's Rāmāyana is on the Assamese society. We find reference in folk literature e.g. Mantras, Biya Nam etc. Mādhab Kandali's Rāma's emotion and activities reflect on Assamese society in various aspects. So, we find great impact of Valmiki's Rāmāyana in our society.

On the other hand, the influence of Rāmāyana in Bengali literature is deep. Because, even in 21th century some Bengali modern litt erateurs had written Rāmāyana. It is appreciable. We Indians feel proud of Rāma's character and we also find our duty, ideology and responsibility through the character of Rāma. After a long time Subhash Bhattacharya translated Valmiki's Rāmāyana to modern Bengali language. He translated the holy epic in prose style in two big volumes. Subhash Bhattacharya claims his work to be the first complete translation of Valmiki's Sanskrit Rāmāyana. There are no elements which are not found in the origin. He translated as it is in the origin to modern Bengli prose style. So, the Rāmāyana of Subhash Bhattacharya has unique value in Rāmāyani Sāhitya.

Hence, I have selected this topic for comparative study of Rāma's character between Mādhab Kandali's Rāmāyana and Subhas Bhattacharya's Valmiki-Rāmāyana. In my paper I discuss the character of Rāma as reflected in these two translation works.

The objectives and aim of research are to stimulate new thinking on some material. Researcher analyses and studies any topic for result which is established with new thinking. Researcher discusses the topics and finds out some special features of those topics. They also challenge previous decisions and establish a new thinking. The topic "A Comparative Study of the Character of 'Rāma' in Mādhab Kandali's Rāmāyana and Subhas Bhattacharya's Bengali Rāmāyana named Valmiki-Rāmāyana" analyses and studies with comparative method. Madhav Kandali and Subhash Bhattacharya sketched the character of Rāma with different points of view. They also analyze and describe the character Rāma. Both of them give concrete shape of Rāma's own choice and ideological side. So, this paper mainly discusses the character of Rāma in these two vernacular writing styles.

The area of this paper mainly focuses on the character of Rāma : how does Mādhab Kandali introduce and describe the character of Rāma vis a vis Subhash Bhattacharya. Hindus believe Rāma is the eighth incarnation of Bishnu. In the origin, Vālmiki describes and introduces the character of Rama as one of the incarnations of Bishnu. But in vernacular edition of Vālmiki's Rāmāyana's, Rāma is not a god. He is as usual human being. Tulsi Das, Kritibash also describe Rāma as a human being, not an incarnation of Bishnu. So, in this paper mainly we study about the character of Rāma with the help of both these two writers.

Character of Rāma

Rāma is the bright character of Vālmiki's Rāmāyana. He is the incarnation of God. The eldest son of Dasarath is Rāma. He is the treasure of goodness of everything. People see so much goodness of his character. For example-he is handsome, obedient, simple, glorious, tolerating of some mistake with smiling face and patience. Vālmiki introduced Rāma as having good character like God.

The Character of Rāma in Mādhab Kandali's Rāmāyana:

The character of Rāma in Madhav Kandali's work is the Supreme Being. Even Brahma and Maheswar bow down to him. He is the cause of creation, existence and destruction of the entire universe. Apramādi poet, Mādhab Kandali has imposed divinity (omnipotence) and greatness in Rāma's character at the very beginning of Ayodhyākānda, (Apramādi means without mistake.) Eg.

Jaya jaya Rāmachandra jagata ādhāra
Brahma Hara Purandara sewak jahar
Sriti sthiti laya jāra lilā anupam
Hen Rāma pade karo sadāy pranām

(Mādhab Kandali: Ramayana, Ayodhyākānda-chepter-1/2, page-92)

(Long Live Ramachandra, the Lord of the Universe Brahma, Hara, Purandara pay regards to Him: The basis of creation and end. Hence, pray to that lord, Rama eternally)

Madhav Kandali has portrayed Rama as the ocean of virtues, full moon etc. It is his characteristic feature that he sees equally whether somebody is his friend and some are foe. All the virtues of God have been amalgamated in Rāma's character. He has no greed for power. He is the beloved not only of Dasaratha, but also of all the inhabitants of Ayodhyā for he can control the enemies like greed, attachment etc. He always bows down to his elders and respected people. The poet has depicted Rāma as a benevolent, forgiving, truthful, righteous, grateful, unbiased and firm character. He is unbiased to all living beings and it is one of the remarkable features of his character. Mādhab Kandali has portrayed Rāma's character from the core of her heart and he has placed Rāma of Vālmiki's Rāmāyana as his role model.

Rama's respect for his father is a unique thing in entirity. Rāma is so strong that he can face any situation. That is why Rāma was not swayed by emotion when he was banished because of the intrigues of Kaikeyi whereas he was about to be consecrated as the heir of Ayodhyā. Rather he continuously paid homage to step mother Kaikeyi who had done wrong to him. This kind of magnanimity of character is incomparable. Rāma revered Kaikeyi more than his own mother. Rāma got pain for Kaikeyi's deeds but did not abuse mother Kaikeyi. Rāma's respect for his father did not diminished, though Dasaratha accepted failure under circumstances and pushed Rāma to near death situations by taking the role of a person, who is conquered by a female. Rather he was prompt in complying to father's decree by giving instance of Parasurāma. Ofcourse, the poet has given boastfulness, proud speech in Rāma's mouth for entertaining people and deviates from the original little bit. The poet has presented Rama's boastfulness and proud speech as follows:

Bapora indrak prati bhaila krodha man
Bandhiya agota dibo tetekshan

...

...

Tribhubana birasame ekesware joro
Durjoy malok sabe dhari ghara foro

..

..

Sata dwipa prithibi rudhimoy kori
Tini satbara furi satriya sanghari
Hena Jamadagni Rama durjoy sarir
kandhata kuthaa age mor bhaila thir

(Mādhab Kandali: Ramayana, chapter-7, Ayodhyākānda, page-103)

Though this kind of speech found in Mādhab Kandali's Rāmāyana has portrayed, Rāma as boastful, proud character, but it is not the fault of this Assamese poet. Because Mādhab Kandali has not depicted Rāma's character as void of boastfulness, pride, ofcourse he has done reverse of it and done this for entertainment of people. He has so much for depicting in Rāma's character that, Rāma's reverence for his future has been reflected in a very lustrous manner. In this regard a comment of Satyenddranāth Sarmāh can be cited.eg. (mulor) Rāmor oktit dambha nai, ātmaslaghā nāi, barang pitri bhaktit ākul putrar bedanā prakāsh paise. Kintu Mādhav Kandaliye seikhini kathar pariborte lok manoranjanarthe Rāmor Mukhat dombhukti, ātmaslaghāpurna bachan diche. Pitrir prati abashye ānugatya hrās karā nāi. (Rāmāyanar Itibritti, page-268)

Rāma of Mādhab Kandali is a super human in most of the times. The charm of his character gets in the verge of losing its beauty for the super human attributes in his manner. Mādhab Kandali's strong creativity has made that too natural. In regard of eagerness for common people, profound respect for father, equal behaviour for friends and foe, benevolence etc. Rāma's character reveals super human attributes.

In Mādhab Kandali's Rāma's character, respect for preceptors has been depicted in a very lustrous manner. Rāma has endless respect for the gurus and sages like Viswāmitra, Vashistha. Rāma has not only made them mentally strong, also protected them from all odds. They have seen the path of salvation in Rāma's shelter. In this respect, Rāma's promise of safeguarding the sages in Dandakāranya from the atrocities of demons and demonesses. In Dandakāranya, the demons had built hills of bones by killing the sages. On seeing this Rāma took the oath of killing the demons and he had done accordingly. From this Rāma's respect for his gurus and his valour can be conjectured.

As Rāma's respect for his father and preceptors is incomparable likewise his forgiveness is also incomparable and worthy to be imitated. As already stated Rama is of that mental caliber that he can leave his seat for even for his enemy. Not to speak of Kaikeyi, even the character of virādha is also to be noted here. Though Virādha deserved the strictest punishment for his cruelty, Rāma actually awarded him with salvation.

Param kripālu guna dekhi o Rāmar
Vārja bairi rākshasar karilanta karma
Dekhā kena iswar bipartite dharma
Nābāsanta jati-kul bhajan mātrake

(Mādhab Kandali: Ramayana, chepter-2, Ayodhyakanda, page-166)

Mādhab Kandali has endowed the character of Rāma with supernaturalism and divinity so as to shield him from the criticism that his actions in relation to Bāli, Rāvana, Shambuka would have otherwise invited.

The poet has the greatest admiration for the character of Rāma which influences his portrayal of the character in favourable light more than in other vernacular translations.

In spite of the divine portrayal of Rāma, the character still retains human interest as in the character we see human feelings of frustration, melancholy, and other human emotions. The expressions of emotions in situations like when Sitā was abducted or was sent to exile or when his father died, bring Rāma down to the level of an ordinary human being stripped of his supernaturalism.

Hence, Rāma has been delineated as God, Super human, supernatural being, idealistic, truthful, courageous, loyal to his parents, without envy, and forgiving in his character and conduct.

The Rāmayana of Subhash Bhattacharya

Bengali literature is recognized all around the world for its treasures. The Bengali scholars and literary figures have written numerous accounts on the great epic. Their poetry, especially the Pālāgān are full of riveting stories and fascinating accounts extracted and inspired from the epic. Till today, in the twenty first century, they have been working on the Rāmāyana. One of the notable translations of the epic into Bengali, done in this century is Subhash Bhattacharya's translation of the Rāmāyana, written in 2016 and published by Bongia Sāhitya Sangsad in prose narrative. The translator has added notes and comments of his own to the text too. The text has not excluded any part of the original text and in that context it is the literal translation of the text. And yet, the text, divided in two volumes has been considered as a great inclusion to the huge collection of works under the single headline of Indian Rāmāyani literature or literature on the Rāmāyana.

Portrayal of Rāma in Subhash Bhattacharya's translation of the Rāmāyana

Bhatthacharya's Rāma is as luminous as Vālmiki's Rāma. Ostentatious rhetoric and contemptuousness are tactfully excluded from his portrayal. Rather, Bhattacharya's Rāma is amicable and kind. Simplicity is the most valued asset in Rama. Hardly any flaw can be traced in the character of Rāma. Moon may carry blemish but Rāma is impeccable. Though the portrait of Rāma is coloured with human emotions, the divinity of the character is not dimmed. In Bhattacharya's portrayal of Rāma, charm is added by the qualities of mercifulness and calmness.

The nobility of the character is enhanced by his resolution. Soft-spoken Rāma is shown to perform all his duties as a prince without any hesitance. Teachings from the artillery trainings were earnestly acquired by Rāma and regularly practiced. In the beginning of the Ayodhyā Kānda, Bhattacharya has described Rāma as:

"Ram chilen rupban o tejoban. Ta charitra chila assuyahin. Pita Dasharather matoi chilen santaprakritir o asheshguna sampan. Sarbadai namra kantha o anuchchakanthe katha balten. ...Rajputra chilen bale nfyamit astravyias karte hata take...jnane bridha tader sange shastradi alosana kare samoy kataten. ...Tine bidwan, bayobridhaor prati shradhasil. Daridra prajabarger prati tini chilen daradi." [Subhash Bhattacharjya: Vālmiki - *Rāmāyana*, Page-133]

(Trans: Rāma was handsome and vigorous. His character was faultless. Like his father Dasaratha, he too was gentle and soft-spoken. He was respectful towards the elders and was kind towards the poverty-stricken citizen of his kingdom.)

Rāma, the immaculate prince is not worthy of a banishment, that too for so long. This injustice is criticized by the ministry and Siddhārtha, the aged minister questions Kaikeyi if there is any rational judgment behind this decision. The noble nature of Rama has inspired all and this flawless prince is admired by all.

"Rame ki pap karechen jar janye take nirbasita katre habe? ...kangka aache chndero kintu ramer charita kalngkashunya." [Subhash Bhattacharjya: Vālmiki - *Rāmāyana*, Page-209]

(Trans: What unlawful has Rāma done for which he is banished? The moon may have flaw but Rāma is flawless.)

In the original text of Rāmāyana too, Rāma is not burdened with any blemish. He is a divine incarnation far from human flaws. His father too has noticed the divine qualities of Ram and being aware of this divinity has affected Dasaratha while announcing his banishment. Later, Dasaratha is found rebuking his wife Kaikeyi as sinful, ruthless and harmful. He describes Rama as:

Je ram ahinhsar pratimurti, kshamashil, tyagi, satyabadi, dharmashilata o kritajnata jar chiritrer anyatom boishitya, sei Ram nathakile amar ki habe." [Subhash Bhattacharjya: Vālmiki - *Rāmāyana*, Page-154]

(Trans: What will happen to me if I lose my self-sacrificing son Ram, the emblem of valuable virtues like non-violence, truthfulness and gratitude?)

Rāma is so resolute that he is not moved even by the strongest emotions of sorrow and pain. He did witness the tearful eyes of his father but he had unseen those mourning and sighs because he must follow the ordeal of the father. Though many distressing thoughts have found their way to his heart, Rāma seems firm. In his mind, he is provoked to question and yet he controls his urge: "Pita ki kono sharik ba maanasik klese klista hachchen? Nirabachchinna such oti durlov. Priyadarshon Bharater athaba shatrughanaor ki amangal hayeche, aamar matara kushale aache to? Rajake asantushata kare, ta aadesh amanya kare kingba tangke kashta diya ek muhurtao banchte chia na ami. Jini sakaler karon, jinni sakshat devote sei mahan pitar birudhacharon ke karbe? Mata, aapni ki krodhbashe ba avimanbashat pitake emon kono ktubakya balechen jar janye tanke emon klishta dekhachche." [Subhash Bhattacharjya: Vālmiki - *Rāmāyana*, Page-170]

(Trans: Father...have you been suffering from any physical pain or mental trauma? Incessant happiness is rare. Are our mothers in good health? Has anything unfortunate happened to my dearest brothers? I would never go against the King or his ordeals. He, who is the divine origin of all, can that father be hurt? Has mother said anything harsh to you? Why do you look so broken, tired and pale?)

In Bhattacharya's Rāmāyana Rāma is as dutiful as in Vālmiki's Rāmāyana. His devoutness is exemplary. For him, the service to his father is the way to heaven. While his mother Koushalyā tries to dissuade him from his duty, it is this devout nature that leads him to remind his mother of her duty as an ideal wife and mother. His foresightedness and devoutness are again seen when he requests his mother to look after his aging father who, he knows is going to suffer from physical illness due to the sorrowful aching heart after banishing Rāma. He says:

In Bhattacharya's Rāmāyana Rāma is as dutiful as in Vālmiki's Rāmāyana. His devoutness is exemplary. For him, the service to his father is the way to heaven. While his mother Koushalyā tries to dissuade him from his duty, it is this devout nature that leads him to remind his mother of her duty as an ideal wife and mother. His foresightedness and devoutness are again seen when he requests his mother to look after his aging father who, he knows is going to suffer from physical illness due to the sorrowful aching heart after banishing Rāma. He says: "patike tyag kare jabar mato nirmamata narir pakshe aar kee-e ba aache. Tai emon nindajanok siddhanta neoa aapnar uchit noi. Aamar jagatpati pita jatadin jibit thakben tatadin tanr sewa karai aapnar chirtan dharma. …aamader uvayer pashkei pitar nirdesh palon kara uchite. Tini aapanar pati, aamar paramguru ebang sakaler pravu. [Subhash Bhattacharjya:Vālmiki - *Rāmāyana*, Page-185]

(Trans: Mother, what can be more brutal for a woman than leaving her husband? Therefore, a slander like this is never expected to happen to you.

Your foremost duty is to lookafter our father till the end. Both of us should devote ourselves to our respective duties. He is your husband, my father and the lord of us all.)

Bhattacharya's Rāma has descended himself from his high, divine stature to humanly nature from time to time. Especially during his lamentations, his human nature glows brighter than the divine nature. His lamentations also provide scopes to prove that Rāma is a man who believes in karma and rebirth. He says:

"Mata Kaushalya purbajanme nichoy anek shreelokoke putra-bichcheder kashta diyesen. Aar sei janye aaj ei durbipak upasthit hayeche. …aar kono matri shrteelok jen aamar moto putrer janma na den, je-putra mayer simahin jantranar karon hayeche. [Subhash Bhattacharjya: Vālmiki - *Rāmāyana*, Page-241]

(Trans: My mother might have punished many women with the bitter pang of separation with their sons in her previous life. That is why now she is suffering from this separation from her son. I pray for no mother to suffer from this unbearable pain of separation from her children.)

Among the engrossing depictions of numerous incidents that occurred during Rāma's stay in Dandakāranya, one is the encounter between Rāma and Virādh. Virādh, the tormented soul was once cursed by Kubera which led to his birth as a demon but he achieved salvation when he meets Rāma. The heart-wrenchingly saddest incident that took place during Rama's stay in Dandakaranya is the abduction of his wife Sitā. Reminiscing the beautiful moments with his beloved wife, Rāma is broken. And this melancholic image of Rāma adds to his human nature.

Each task and turmoil done and experienced by Rāma is presented skillfully in the poetic prose of Bhattacharya. His soulful treatment of Rāma has made the prose equally fascinating as the poetic treatment of Rāma in Vālmiki's Rāmāyana. Rāma is extremely firm in his decision of testing Sitā's purity and chastity and then banishing her. He is conscious and fearful towards the society where he has been living. To satisfy the society, he has attempted such ruthlessness towards his wife. This impartial, dispassionate treatment towards all has towered Rāma in the ivory tower of divinity. He is a selfless, sober, amiable and honorable divine being; he is a noble man with qualities unattainable to human being in general.

The difference between Madhav Kandali's Rāmāyana and Subhash Bhattacharya's portrayal of Rāma

Both the scholars of Rāmāyana have situated Rāma as the central character of the epic but the treatment of Rāma is noticeably distinct in both the text. A comparison and contrast of the two portrayals of Rāma are discussed briefly:

1. Kandali has described Rāma as the highest authority of the universe, with whose blessings one may achieve divine grace; the devotion of Rāma will lead to salvation. Bhattacharya too has attempted to portray Rāma as a divine being but he has not invited his readers to attain salvation through praying Rāma.
2. Both have portrayed Rāma as the dutiful, obedient, amicable son who is always ready to follow his father's order. Ram is seen as responsible and subordinate towards his father. Rāma is found reminding his mother of her duties as well.
3. Ram is valiant and strong in both texts of the Rāmāyana. The divine order respects him. He is the victor of the world.
4. Rāma in both the texts is seen as truthful, intelligent, respectful towards his elders and religious.
5. He believes in karma and rebirth. He is a devout believer of fortune and luck.
6. The heart-wrenching lamentations have made Rāma more human in both the texts.
7. Through incidents like Bāli-badh and Rāvana-badh, the supernatural qualities of Rāma are focused on.
8. In Kandali's Rāmāyana, the trial by fire that Sitā had to face, known as Agni-parikshā has descended Rāma to the level of a mere human being who is driven by strong passion of rage. Here the pride and suspicion of Rāma is bluntly expressed. The battle with Ravana is actually an attempt to establish his masculinity in the society.

We see the similarities in Rāma's character in Mādhab Kandali and Subhash Bhattacharjya's translated Rāmāyana. But some differences are found in Rāma's character in both writers translated Rāmāyana. Discussed are the differences of Rāma's character between both translated Rāmāyana below:

1. Mādhab Kandali has delineated Rāma categorically as God, whereas Subhash Bhattacharrya does not give Rāma the same stature.
2. In every episode kandali prescribes chanting Rāma's name as the panacea for all evils and troubles of human life, and the passport to the release from kaliyug. But this is absent in Bhattacharrya.s depiction.
3. Bhattcharyya presents the expression of lament and sadness of Rāma quite extensively. While in Kandali there is no such exaggeration but brevity and moderation in depicting the same.
4. Kandali's Rāma imagines enemies or opponents like Indra to be the cause of Dasaratha's sadness prior to his anointment as the prince,

while Bhattacharrya's Rāma speculates that the sadness could be due to his (Rāma's) fault or Kaikeyi emotionally hurting the King.

Conclusion

The influence of Rāmāyana on Indian life and society has been immense from time immemorial to the present times. It was in the 14th century that Rāmāyana studies initiated in Assam thanks to Madhav Kandali. In Bangla literature starting from Tulsi Das to the contemporary, Subhash Bhattacharrya, Rāmāyana studies have continued. Both Kandali and Bhattacharrya have beautifully presented the greatness, valour and glory of the character of Rāma. However, it is in the Bhattacharya's Rāmāyana that the human aspects of the great Rāma have been far more emphasized.

Bibliography

1. Bhattacharjya, Subhash: Vālmiki - Rāmāyana, First Published-Mahālayā 2016 Publisher-Debashis Bhattacharjya, Bangiya Sāhitya Sangsad, Kolkata-09, Volume-1&2
2. Goswami, Indira: Rāmāyana from Gangā to Brahmaputra, First Published-1996, Publisher-B.R. Publishing Corporation, Delhi-052
3. Kandali, Mādhab: Sapta Kanda Ramayana, Reprint-July 2009, Publisher-Ananta Hāzarikā, Dibrugarh-1
4. Sarmā, Shashi: Mādhab Kandali Rāmāyana, Fifth Edition-december-2011, Publisher-Journal Emporium, Nalbari-01
5. Sarmā, Satyendranāth: Rāmāyanar Itibriti, Second Edition-1989, Publisher-Bina Libray, Ghy-01

Chapter XVI

Ramayan-The Sri Lankan Stage Performance

W.M. Amila Damayanthi

The Rama Sitha story is highly popular among the people in Sri Lanka. Sinhala and Tamil community has a wide knowledge about Ramayan. Folklore about Ramayan can be heard from Sabaragamuwa, Eastern and Central Mountain areas in Sri Lanka. Instead of that, many places can be found related to Sitha and Hanuman in different area in the country. Also, folk dramas based on Rama Sitha story can be found in area closer to Batticaloa in Eastern province. Folk theatre tradition called Kuttu, is popular among the people around Batticaloa, still depicting Rama Sitha story in their theatre performances. Non folk theatre called "Noorthi", popular as "Theatre", developed at the end of 18th century was also presented Rama Sitha story on an elaborated theatres[1]. That became an exclusive theatre experience for people in that era. Those theatre performances were having more than 60 songs and the length of the performance was about three hours[2]. Three stories influenced by Rama Sitha legend exis in Noorthi style[3] Maha Ramayana, Sitha Haranaya and Uththara Rama Charithaya. Intention of this research report is to give an idea about, how Ramayana was represented in dramatic way in Noorthi tradition, how the reaction of the audience was then and now, and how Ramayanaya is depicted in local theatre as a theatre performance.

Until the beginning of 19th century, Sri Lankans used to entertain themselves by watching Kolam, Sokari and Nadagam[4]. Rather than kolam and sokari, the theatre style influences from south Indian dance and music called Nadagam was popular among people until the end of 19th century[5]. Popularity of those theatre traditions were totally collapsed at the end of 19th century, with the arrival of the theatre tradition introduced by Baliwaala Percy Victoriya Theatre Companyin 1880. The local audience was amazed to see those performances[6]. The context due to discuss in this research report also started after the arrival of those theatre companies. Therefor, revealing the history regarding that topic is highly necessary. The Percy theatre artists were famous as theatre veteran who performed their theatres in south and north India in 19th century. But, presenting deep appreciations, own identities and rich humanities were not in their performances[7]. Those performances were providing ruff, lethargic entertainment. Because of their dance, music, singing, stage decorations, magic actions, makeup and elaborated costumes, Indian and Sri Lankan audiences got attracted to their performances. People felt they were witnessing an amazing theatre performance they have never seen before.

Baliwaala Percy Victoria company started to perform their theatres at Crytereance Hall in Maradana in 1st January 1977[8]. Language of their theatre was Urdhu and North Indian Classical Music was used as music. Love stories were mostly presented and they were also three hours long.The stage technology was very new and it was a new experience for local audience. Petrol match lamps used in their theatres were covered with multi coloured filters. The audience who witnessed "Indra Sabha" drama performed on 1st January 1917, was mesmerized by the glamour of it and started watching all the other dramas. 26 dramas were presented from January to March1917 on different days and Ramayanaya was stage twice on 3rd and 8th of February 1917[9]. As a result of that,theatre loving people from Colombo, started creating similar dramas. Intention of them was to present Sri Lankan stories using Percy style. Those dramas presented in new style unique from Nadagam or other folk dramas, they called Noorthi for purpose of recognising[10].

John De Silva was the first Sri Lankan who tried Rama Sitha story in Noorthi style. John De Silva has a special place among Sinhalese artist. It is not an exaggeration to say there are no other dramatists comparative to John De Silva in Sinhalese theatre. He was called the Father of Sinhalese theatre, Sinhalese Shakespeare and Sri Lankan Kaalidasa. He was popular not only among drama lovers, he was even popular among the people who have never visited a theatre in their lives[11]. John De Silva was a member of C. Don Bastian's drama company. In 1885 he started his own theatre company called Ceylon Oriental Dramatic Company Limited and wrote six dramas for his company[12]. Two of them were influence by Rama Sitha story. Those were "Lanka Dhawaanor Mahaa Raamayanaya" and "Sitha Haranaya or Ginigath Ramayanaya". Later, he wrote "Uththara Rama Charithaya". Those scripts were written in deep Sinhala and Sanskrit words were used often in those. They had songs with fabulous lyrics. Those dramas were advertised as Noorthi followed by Percy style dramas. In that era, Percy style dramas that were considered as dramas provided cheap entertainment for urban people in India. Influences of Western Realistic dramas and Eastern Western Musical Dramas were clearly visible in those dramas[13]. They were similar to carnivals with dance music and singing. John De Silva was not happy about those Identities of Percy drama style and he was mixing Sanskrit drama style with Percy style to create a new drama tradition. We can't say his effort was successful. But as a result, he managed to create a new theatre style with a strong artistic approach[14]. Rama Sitha story was also presented in that new drama style.

The greatest drama of John De Silva out of Rama Sitha Stories can mentioned as Sitha Haranaya or Ginigath Ramayanaya. It was the first drama which Sinhalese audience experienced in a proscenium theatre related to Ramayanaya. It was performed in theatre called "Pushpa Shala" in 31st March 1886[15]. Description of this drama can be extracted as this.

"This is publishing for low prize because there are many information about old Sir Lanka written in the story of Ramayanaya by saint Waalmiki and it is important for Sinhalese people to know about those things. Therefore Sitha Haranaya is bringing on to the local stage by following the footsteps of Naatya Shasraya as a drop of immense Ramayanaya[16]."

People started believing this story has a bad luck even before it was premiered. Proving that belief, after the premier Pushpa Shaala theatre got burnt. Later it was found out that it was done by somebody because of the jealousy[17]. But people believed that happened because of the super natural power of Rama and Rawana. Later the same drama was staged as Ginigath Ramayana or Burnt Ramayanaya. Summary of Sitha Haran Noorthi can be described in this way18. It was staged in three episodes. This was mentioned as "Jananee Harana".

First Act

- Prince Rama used to play with his bow and arrow and shoot birds in his garden. Ones he was playing in the garden and a lady with a hunched back was walking across the garden. Rama shot an arrow to that lady to annoy her. When the arrow hits the lady, her hunch back disappeared. But, the lady was angry with Rama about his misbehaviour. She went to Queen Kaike and influenced her to claim the throne of the Kingdom to her son instead of giving it to crown prince Rama.
- Meanwhile, female demon Thadaka was interrupting the meditation of rhishi Wishwamitra in his monastery. Rhishi made a request to king Dasharatha to send his son Rama to his monastery to punish Thadaka. At the beginning the king was not happy about Wishwamitra's request. But later he agreed to send his sons Rama and Laskhmana together with rhishi Wishwamithra.

- Then Rama killed the female demon Thadaka.
- When he was returning back to his kingdom he saw Sitha, daughter of King Janaka from Mithila kingdom and fell in love with her.

Second Act

- When Rama Lakshman and rhishi Whishwamitra are in Janakapura, King Janaka challenged Rama to show his talents by bending a bow. King promised to let Rama marry his daughter if he bends the bow. Rama did it and claimed Sitha as his wife.
- Conversation in between Sitha and king Janaka.
- Queen Kaike claiming the throne for her son Bharatha from King Dasharatha and Rama is offering the throne to his younger brother Bharatha and leaving the kingdom with Sithe and Lakshmana to Dandaka forest in south India.
- In Dandaka forest Rama is meeting rhishi Aghasthi and he is saying Dandaka forest is threatened by demons from Sri Lanka.
- Meanwhile Ravana's sister Suparnaka approaching Lakshmana and asking to marry her. Lakshmana getting angry with Suparnaka and cut her nose and her breast.

Third Act

- Suparnaka is going to Rawana and saying a different story. She is saying she saw a beautiful lady in Dhandaka forest and she is with full of beauty as a goddess. She was trying to bring that lady to Ravana but Lakshmana came and cut Suparnakas nose and Breast.
- Rawana is angry and ordering minister Maricha to transform himself as a golden deer and go to Dhandaka Forest. Sitha sees the golden deer and ask Rama to bring it to her. Rama goes to bring the golden deer and Lakshmana follows him.
- Meanwhile, Rama comes with his Dandu Monara and kidnapping Sitha.
- Rama is realizing his beloved Sitha is missing. Meanwhile, Hanumana the son of goddess Anjanan comes to help Rama and bringing Rama's ring with him to Sri Lanka to find Sitha.

Fourth Act

- Hanumana kills Ravana's guardians and, meet Sitha in Ashoka forest. Showing Rama's ring to Sitha. Bringing Sithas ring back to Rama.
- Conversation in between Sitha and Thrijata.

- ❖ Ravana is showing his lustful love to Sitha. And Sitha refuse his proposal.
- ❖ Ravana and Lakshmana come with an immense army of monkeys and Sri Lankans were informing that to king Ravana.

Fifth Act

- ❖ Ravanas brother Vibheeshana inviting Rama for peace talk and Rama agrees.
- ❖ Ravana and Vibheeshana arguing with each other and angry Vibheeshana joining Ramas side.
- ❖ Fight between Ravanas son Indrajith and Hanuman. Indrajith showing a fake head and saying Sitha died and this is her head. Hanuma became sad to see the head and Vibheeshana says to Hanuman it is a fake head.
- ❖ Hanuman kills Indrajith.
- ❖ War between Rama and Ravana. And Rama kills Ravana.
- ❖ God Shakra comes and explaining the loyalty of Sitha.
- ❖ Rama leaves to India with Sitha and handing over Lankapura to Vibheeshana.

Noorathy of Sithaharanaya including those five acts.The cast of this Noorthi drama was as mentioned below. King Dashsratha, King Janaka, Prince Lakshmana, Prince Bharatha, Rhishi Wishwamithra, Washishta, Aghasthi, Hanuma, Ravana, Vibheeshana, Indrajith, Mareecha, Sitha (Janaki), Kaike, Thadaka, Suparnaka, Khuni and Shakra.[19]

Using different backdrops painted beautifully with colour full sceneries as, flower gardens, inner chamber of Dhasharatha palace, flower garden of Mithila region, King Janaka's palace in a street of Mithila region, full view of the palace of king Janaka, Dhandaka forest, Ravanas palace and war field are hanging behind the stage. There are descriptions on the backdrops regarding the place of the act. This came to Noorthi from the influence of Percy drama style.

Drama means briefly, a story between raising a conflict and solving the conflict. Ramayanaya and Sithaharanaya Noorthi are completed with above mentioned norms of dramas. First of all, dramatists are giving an introduction and knowledge about the environment of the story's background, characters and relationships between the each other. Then his focus is to create a background to build up a conflict between those characters or to pave a path towards a clash between them. Desires of the leading role Rama and the villain Ravana are clashing together. Then the attention of the audience is focusing on that. This incident is carefully created in Great Ramayanaya. Hanumantha fighting with Ravana's guardians. Then he fights with Indrajith. As this the conflict is rising to the peak that means the beginning of war between Rama and Ravana. With the death of Ravana, tension of the audience is released.

The music used in Noorthi related to Rama Sitha story was kept in high standard.

John de Silva, the author of those dramas, was a person with a great knowledge of music, poet, music critic and a person who introduced classical Indian music to Sri Lanka[20]. He wrote 61 songs for Great Ramayana and composed music for those songs using north Indian classical ragas. Thus most of the songs were created using peelu, bheirava, kafi, bheiravi, bhupali, kamaj, yeman ragas. Beats from trithal, keherva, chauthal were used as the beats of those songs. The songs of Sithaharanaya staged in 1886 are still popular among people in Sri Lanka. "Amba damba naran, Sriya manmath vee ma, Sitha ma siriya" song can be taken as an example to prove it. Until today, those songs are popular among general community in Sri Lanka. Drama means creating story using an incident. Because of that,script writers are showing an interest in dramatic incidents. But the dramas with story of Sitha and Rama was showing more interest to present songs than those dramatic incidents. But doubtfulness, tension and surprise was also included in Rama Sitha Noorthi. Great Ramayana Noorthi showing sub incidents of the story, is helping to develop the selected major incidents more dramatic and meaningful.Because, dramatist have chosen only the dramatic incidents from Vaalmiki's Great Ramayan poem.

There are two drama methods according to Bharathamuni's popular descriptions, Loka dharmi (Realistic), Natyadharmi (Non-realistic). The Noorthi depicting Rama Sitha story is representing the non- realistic category. Dramatists are expecting to present the story in imaginary way than showing it in realistic way inthis drama method. Drama, music and singing are essential components in those dramas. Ramayanaya, Sithaharanaya, Great Rama character Noorthi are rich visually and musically. Noorthi also fits in to the Sanskrit drama structure, because it is also goes in to the dimensions of 5 major incidents as Arambha, Yathna, Prapthyasha, Niyathapthi, and Palasama similar to Sanskrit dramas. But it is not so prominent as in Sanskrit dramas. Presenting incidents using songs rather than dialogues can be seen in Noorthi very often, but sometimes the dialogues from day to day life are also included in the script. Costumes and ornaments of Rama, Seethe Noorthi remind costumes of ancient kings. They were dressed up with elaborated costumes and ornaments. Those costumes were made related to Indhu Arya tradition and imitating "English, Roman, Persian and Mogul" costumes for the decorations. Dramatists expect attraction of the audience by dressing up actors and actresses with elaborated costumes. Prince Rama is having a yellowish brown dhoti and having shawl and garlands. Sometimes he is also wearing a small crown. Sitha is having a red jacket and a red dhoti, having flowers on her head and wearing jewellery. Ravana's makeup was with a cruel appearance. Wearing a Jacket and a dhoti with Blue, Black, Yellow and Red colours, along with a crown. Wearing authentic ornaments is suitable for a king. Dark colours were used for face makeup. Backdrops were displayed behind the stage according to the scene. It will provide an idea about the scene. Using modern technology for backdrop and stage settings was one speciality of Noorthi. Among stage decors, king's court of Ravana, Throne and the palace of king Janaka are highlighted. Bows and arrows of Rama and Lakshmana, Hanuman's Yagadha, Swards, Blades, Spheres, Pitchers are used as props. By analysing and watching Noorthi dramas, written in Sinhalese, it is visible that the intention of the author was to create a Noorthi using Ramayanayana written by Vaalmiki. According to the Indian beliefs, prince Rama is worshiped as a god. But in Sri Lanka people are not worshiping Rama as a god. Only a contradiction exists regarding Ravana. After presenting this story as Sithaharanaya in 31st may 1886, by John de Silva, it was reproduced as Maha Ramayanaya (The Great Ramayana) in 1971. Later as a result of rebuilding Noorthi tradition again, Towerhall foundation produced and Lionel Goonathilake directed the same Noorthias "Ramayanaya"on 25 January 2017. This was staged many times in different locations of the country. Intention of that performance was to re-establish the Noorthi tradition instead of promoting devotions for Rama and Sitha.The opinion of modern viewers was Ravana should not be represented as a cruel demon. Because modern Sri Lankans are believing Ravana was a religious ruler, a doctor, a person with broad knowledge of technology and nature a lover. Therefore, Ravana's death at the end of the performance was not proving happiness for them. As a whole Noorthi depicting Rama Sitha stories have specialities, mentioned below:-

1. Sharp moments of Rama Sitha stories was compressed in to a 3 hour performance.
2. Dialoguase of the whole story were boosted up with songs.
3. Combination of the scenes are amazingly matched.
4. The Proscenium stage that was used was admirable.
5. Containing an eternal pleasure, it is was able to attract the audience until today.

Prestigious, personality and heroism, unrestrained nature, active manner of Rama, unmeasurable loyalty of Sitha was carefully represented in Ramayanaya

Noorthi. That means it was trying to raise a new meaning to the humanity. In this story Suparnaka was represented as a sinful and lustful woman. Ravan was represent as a greedy person. Sitha highlighted as a soft hearted, self-esteemed woman. But with the audience feedback, it is visible that they were expecting only an entertainment by watching this story rather than getting a motivation.

References

1. Sunil Ariyarathne - John De Silva - Noorthi Natya Ekathuwa (Collection of Noorthy drama), (4th half) 2008, S. Godage Publication, page 49
2. P.W Jayantha - John De Silva Lipi Saraniya:Noorthi Sangeethaya, 2009, Tower hall theatre foundation, page 57
3. Vimal Disanayaka - John De Silva Saha Sinhala Natya, 2009, Tower hall theatre foundation publication, page 19-20
4. Vimal Disanayaka - John De Silva Saha Sinhala Natya, 2009, Tower hall theatre foundation publication, page 23
5. Ediriweera Sarachchandra - Sinhala Gaminatakaya,1992, National Education Institute, page 182
6. Wimal Disanayaka - John De Silva Saha Sinhala Natya, 2009, Tower hall theatre foundation publication, page 21
7. Same, page 20
8. Thissa Kariyawasam - 20 Years of Sinhala Drama and Theatre Art, 2012, S. Godage Publication, page 28-29
9. Same, page 28-29
10. Ediriweera Sarachchandra - Sinhala Gaminatakaya 1992, National Education Institute, page 183
11. Wimal Disanayaka - John De Silva Saha Sinhala Natya, 2009, Tower hall theatre foundation publication, page 09
12. Ven. Theripaha Somananda - John De Silva Articles : Socialand Religious concepts of John de Silva, 2009, Tower hall theatre foundation publication, page 14
13. Thissa Kariyawasam - 20 Years of Sinhala Drama and Theatre Art, 2012, S. Godage Publication, page 32
14. Wimal Disanayaka - John De Silva Saha Sinhala Natya, 2009, Tower hall theatre foundation publication, page 30
15. I. Sunil Ariyarathne - John De Silva - Noorthi Natya Ekathuwa, (4th half), 2008, S. Godage Publication, page 49

    II. Dramatist John de Silva - Department of National Archives, 1986, Page 05
16. Same, page 49
17. Same, page 49
18. Same, pages 50-53
19. Same, page 82
20. Wimal Disanayaka - John De Silva Saha Sinhala Naatya, 2009, Tower hall theatre foundation publication, page 57

Chapter XVII

Ramayana Tradition in Thailand : Miniature Painting and Khon Masks

Chariya Dharmboon

Thai people know "Ramakien" literature accordingly although they may not know all stories. But at least, they understand the the story in brief (refered to Pra Ram followed Sida and brought her back from Tosakan; king of giants,who has ten heads and twenty hands. Monkey army was on Pra Ram's side. Hanuman (white monky) was a brave soldier who is needed and played a big role widely. As a matter of Ramakien (Thai version), King Rama I took the original from the Ancient India Literature which was composed by Valmiki Ramayana. This is the Hindu prose in sanskrit called "ślok". This can be classified into 7 chapter that comprised of "Balakan, Ayodhayakan, Aranyakan, Kisakintakan, Sunthornkan, Yudhakan and Uttarakan.

Ramakien in Thai style and Ramayana of India differ in many parts such

- Tosakan means person who has ten necks or ten heads, India called Ravana, Ravan or Rap
- Sida Sita in India
- Pra Lak Luxaman in India
- Phiphek Phiphisana in India
- Nang Montho (giant's king wife) Monthodhari in India
- In Ramayana, Ravana or Rap was the son of Wisarap.

He was Brahmin inherited by Brahma and Nang Kaiyakesi) (daughter of krung Longka'king). This is different from Ramakien. Tosakan was the demon son of King Lustian (the ruler of Longka) and Nang Rachada. For the sake of IndiaN epic, the father of Rap was the powerful Brahmin resulting from Brahma. The reason for giving birth to giant because Giant Sumalee (Longka's ruler) let daughter married Wisarap. This deed expects for future nephew will derive power from Brahma. He was Rap,Ravana or Tosakan.

- The birth of Tosakan in Ramayana, the previous life Tosakan and Kumpakan keep an eye on Pra Narai (Visnu) heaven. One day the hermit came to visit Pra Narai, both of them don't allow anyone to see in accordance with Pra Narai's command. The hermit cursed both to gain torture in the human world and Pra Narai couldn't remove the curse. When both were born as Asura or giant, he'll disguise escaping from torture. As of Ramakien (Thai version) originated from giant named Nonthok who has duty on washing angels' feet at footstep of mount Krailas. He was teased by hair pulling until he was bald. Therefore, he prayed for blessing from Isvara god to have diamond fingers which can point to death. When he got, he was crazy and pointed angels to death. This behavior effects Pra Narai to disguise as beautiful angel to tease Nonthok to dance until he pointed himself to death. Before Nonthok died, he saw Pra Narai was back to the God figure with 4 hands. So, he mocked that Pra Narai has 4 hands to bully. Pra Narai commanded Nonthok to reborn with 10 heads, 20 hands and he'll be born as human with 2 hands to kill him. According to this, Nonthok was reborn as Tosakan and Pra Narai disguised as Pra Ram and Luxmi (Pra Narai's wife) incarnated as Nang Sida (couple of Pra Ram). Later, it caused The Ramakien great war which resulted in large number of giants' death.

- The miracle of Nang Sida began at birth because Rosalyn (Tosakan) fell in love and kidnapped Nang Sida. When Nang Montho (the mother : Tosakan's wife), when Nang Montho gave birth to daughter, the baby cried "planlap" it's mean "kill giant" for 3 times. Giant astrologers interfered with Phiphek (Tosakan's brother) predicted that the baby will devastate ethnic of giants. This is necessary for Tosakan to float baby. Prachanok hermit found and brought her back. But the hermit status was inappropiate to raise baby, he buried the golden casket and begged for Mother Earth to take care instead. Then Prachanok hermit resigned from hermit status to rule Mithila Nakorn, he harrowed, pulled casket and opened it. He found Nang Sida grew up and she was so beautiful, he accepted as daughter and named "Sida" which means furrows. Next, he held the finding couple marriage by arrow lifting competition or Mahadhanu Moli. Pra Ram was triumphant and married Nang Sida. Sida in Valmiki epic was the daughter of Pra Phumee or Mother Earth, she was born in the earth. When Prachanok (Mithila's king) performed ploughing and harvesting ceremony, then accepted as daughter and held the finding couple marriage by arrow lifting competition as Ramakien story.

Ram or Pra Ram (ram) was the main actor in Ramakien. Pra Ram was the seventh sector of Pra Narai (Visnu God) "Ramavatar" or Ramachandravatar Incarnate as King Tossaratha'son and Nang Kao Suriya. He had green colour body and armed with arrows. There are three magical arrows ranging from Sorn Prommart, Sorn Palaiwat and Sorn Agniwat. This will appear four hands with weapons Three-jagged (Tri]¢xUl), Wand (Kathag/a), Mach (Chakra)[1]) and Conch (Sung). Pra Ram's body was light green with one head and two hands wearing Pramah mongkut. He has three brothers with the same father. They are Pra Prot (sanskrit "Bharata"), Pra Lak (sanskrit "Laksaman") and Pra Sattrut (sanskrit "Sattarut"). Pra Ram's wife was Nang Sida (daughter of Tosakan with Nang Montho), they have a son called "Pra Mongkut) and military post called "Hanuman"

Pra Ram in Thai belief-Thai people believe that the king incarnated from Pra Narai (Visnu God). The name of the king always will be "Ram", for example, the king of Sukhothai period named "Ramkamhaeng", Ayudhaya period named had Somdej Pra Ramadhibodi I (king U-Thong), Rattanakosindra period Chakri dynasty (Chak-Tri, Pra Narai weapon): ther were beginning of the king's name in each reign was Somdej Pra Ramadhibodi for instance, Prabat Somdej Pra Ramadhibodi IX or Prabat Somdej Pra Paramintaramaha Bhumipol Adulyadej Boromnathbopit.

Otherwise, popularity of Pra Ram had been expanded to people as artwork. We can notice obviously through Ramakien mural paintings at the Emerald Buddha Monastery or Wat Pra Kaew. They painting were different from the former. Generally, Thai mural painting was written about Buddha history or 10 Jataka tales. This concerned with previous life of Lord Buddha. Before he was born as a king and ordained until he had enlightenment, mural paintings in these topics provided as Buddha worshippers. Ramakien's mural painting at the Emerald Buddha Monastery, on the contrary, as its base was written with based on Ramayana of India.

King Rama I had been pleased to erect the Emerald Buddha together with Bangkok Metropolitance in 1782 to locate Pra Mahamanee Rattanapatimakorn or Pra Kaew Morakot (Thai priceless Buddha statue). Ramakien's mural paintings was written during the 3rd reign (Prabat Somdej Pra Nangklao) to cerebrate King Rama I as Ramakien composer by referring from the fomer outline "Ramayana". Ramakien mural paintings around the balcony were started with Narai's incarnated before being born as Pra Rama. This can be observed around the door corner and on the top of balcony. There are 80 pics appoximately followed with Ramakien from room 1-178 with subtitle and poem description, inscripted on the marble surrounding the balcony.

Furthermore, Pra Ram appraisal is displayed in "Khon" which will perform "Ramakien". The story involves humankind, non-human and angels (Demon and Angel). There was a role play that created characters similar to

"Khon" in the story which led to Khon masks, to encourage appreciation of the performer and the audience. Thus, Khon mask is crucial in performing "Khon"

Khon mask background: This is supposed that the origin of "Khon performing" had been displayed without masks. Colour painting on face for each performer was done relate to character like "Kathakkali" of India. But Khon performing divided many actors and make-up artist. (By this reason, the idea of creating miniature "khon" mask in various forms by covering head instead). Khon mask, used in performing Ramakien will classify characters through face apperance, role and status, can be observed by head wearings which will seperate in lower or higher level consecutively of each "khon". Moreover, face will be painted in different colour for audience to memorize easily.

Khon mask classification: In order to understand stories during performance can divided into 3 categories:

1. Face Division
   - 1.1 Human and Angel mask
   - 1.2 Non-human mask
   - 1.3 Monkey and others animals
2. Khon mask accessories adornment classification
   - 2.1 Longka city side or giants wearing the crown topped with variety of accessories.
   - 2.2 Plapla side was monkey seperation
3. Face characters of khon masks come in colour group (red, yellow, violet, indigo, green, black, grey and brown)

Khon masks format

Ramakien is liture which comprises of many performers called "Bhongsa" or "Vangsa" as thess :

- Bhongsa Narai (visnu) include kings of Ayudhaya city and orthers regions, such as Pra Lak, Nang Sida, King Tossaros, Pra Prot and Pra Sattarut
- Brahma Bhongsa and Giant Bhongsa krung Longka consist of Brahma (krung Longka settler), the 1th king, king of giant, giant soldiers, for instance, Tosakan, Phiphek, Indarachit, Benjaguy and giant sea butterfly (Pee Sua Samut)
- Mahesvara Bhongsa is god, angels, Pra Isaun,Pra Narai, Viganesh, Pra Agni
- Mongky Bhongsa include king of monkeys, monkey with 18 crowns, monkey soldiers (Hanuman, Sukreep, Ongkot)

These Khon masks are not only for covering head for hiding real face of performers but also being Thai prestige art with knowledge and ultimate skills. Procedure will be handled by Thai criftsman along with longevity and intellectual wisdom.

Conclusion

Popularity in Ramayana of Thai people appear apparently in daily life. These can be found in many kinds of mural paintings in monastery. Khon masks were produced for performing Ramakien will seperate as prestige art. Performers have to pass thraift intense selection and hard-working in rehearsal. Khon mask created by many of craftsman, these processes are very important part remaining reputation and honorary eternally.

Author Address

Dr. Juri Gogoi Konwar	: Dept. of Cultural Studies, Tezpur University, Napaam, Tezpur-784028, Assam e-mail : jgkon@tezu.ernet.in
Dr. Moushumi Kandali	: Assistant Professor, Department of Cultural Studies, Tezpur University, Tezpur, Assam
Dr. Ranjan Chakravarty	: Associate Professor, K. K. Handique Govt. Sanskrit College, Guwahati-781014, Assam
Sarat Kr. Doley	: Assistant Professor of English, Department of English and Foreign Languages, Tezpur University, Assam
Saurva Sengupta	: Damdama College, Kulhati
Gakul Kumar Das	: Darrang College, Tezpur, Assam
Dr. Hari Prasad Baruah	: Assistant professor, Dept. of Assamese Lokanayak Omeo Kumar Das College, Assam
Muktar Ali	: Assistant professor, Dept. of Hindi Lokanayak Omeo Kumar Das College, Assam
Prof. (Dr.) Jyotsna K.B. Rout	: Department of M.I.L & L.S., Director-in-Charge, Centre For Languages and Cultural Studies, Gauhati University, Guwahati, Mobile No : 09706880088 e-mail : jyotsnarout@rediffmail.com

Kalpana Agarwala	:	Student (IDOL), Gauhati University, Assam, Mobile No : 8876536396 e-Mail : maramikanu@gmail.com
Lina Devi	:	Research Scholar, Gauhati University, Assam
Pratibha Tomar	:	Assostant Professor, Department of English, Tinsukia Commerce College. Tinsukla, Assam
Rupanjoli Hazarika	:	Assistant Professor Dept. of English, Suren Das College, Haj
Dr. Pratima Pallai **Dr. Sashapra Chakrawarty**	:	Assistant Professors, Department of Education, School of Humanities and Social Science, Tezpur University, Assam
Dr. Subhra Sabhapandit	:	Assistant Professor, Department of Sanskrit, Handique Girls College, Guwahati-781001, Assam
Tina Sarma	:	Research Scholar, Department of Sanskrit, Gauhati University, Assam
Dr. Dulal Chandra Das	:	Assistant Professor, HOD, Department of Assamese, Darrang College
W.M. Amila Damayanthi	:	Hindi Instructor, (B.A, M.A, D.A, PGDC) Faculty of Dance and Drama University of Visual and Performing Arts Colombo 07, Sri Lanka
Chariya Dharmaboon	:	Lecturer (History of Art), College of Fine Arts

❑❑